Praise for The Art of Your Energy

"I had a total hip replacement 1.5 years ago. When the other hip started to hurt and caused me to limp, I became very concerned. I was worried that I'd have to go through another replacement. When I started receiving Mari's living light codes not only did the pain go away but I stopped limping and it has not returned. Mari's codes are truly miraculous and a divine blessing!"

-Kathleen M.

"These blessed codes have changed my life. I feel amazing after they are energetically placed where needed in my system. I believe these are a true godsend and I will forever be using these symbols whenever I feel necessary."

-Melanie L.

"I have been working with Mari for a couple years now and ever since she incorporated the light codes, it has been incredibly transformative in my work as a healer and my life as a whole. I definitely feel an effect on a mental, emotional, spiritual and physical level. Mari is absolutely amazing, and the addition of the light codes has elevated her skill for any situation. It is truly a gift to be able to work with Mari!"

-Kirsty D.

"My new hand therapist and current physical therapist are very surprised by how much function I have in my shoulder and arm so soon after surgery. The light code healing is definitely working! It seems as if I may avoid more surgery as the nerves are regenerating on their own!"

-Lois S.

"I've known Mari for a few years now and she has helped me with various issues that I've had in the past. So in 2020 when I was diagnosed with cancer it was pretty much a no brainer to contact Mari and ask for help. August 2020 my left kidney was removed and I began working with Mari as soon as I got out of the hospital. I was admitted on Tuesday morning. I went home Wednesday evening. I don't take drugs so with Mari's help I was able to manage recovery quite well. By September, I had started chemotherapy. As I am fairly stubborn, I was convinced that I was going to work after my first chemo treatment. I dressed for work in my shirt and tie and did my first chemo treatment. When I stood up from the chemo chair, I knew I was not going to make it to work. The chemo treatment I was on was a five-drug chemo cocktail which pretty much just sucked the life out of me. Again working with Mari to have energy to make it to work, I was able to work all the way through my chemo treatments and only missed a couple of days. I contribute this all to Mari's help."

-Brian G.

"I had a torn meniscus; my knee was hot and swollen. After the codes were sent, the pain went away completely, and I am walking fine."

-Missy M.

THE *art* OF YOUR ENERGY

ANGELIC & GALACTIC HEALING AND REGENERATIVE LIGHT CODES

MARI BECKMAN
ILLUSTRATIONS BY THOM BECKMAN

Copyright ©2021 by Mari Beckman

All rights reserved.

This book or part thereof may not be reproduced in any form by any means, electronic or mechanical, including photocopy, recording, or otherwise, or by any information storage and retrieval system, except as may be expressly permitted in writing from the publisher as provided by the United States of America copyright law. Requests for permission should be addressed to Doce Blant Publishing, Attn: Rights and Permissions Dept., 1600-B Dash Point Road, #1040, Federal Way, WA 98023

Published by

Doce Blant Publishing, Federal Way, WA, 98023
www.doceblantpublishing.com

Cover by Fiona Jayde Media
Illustrations and interior art by Thomas Beckman

Paperback ISBN: 978-1-955413-00-8
Spiral ISBN: 978-1-955413-01-5

Library of Congress Control Number: 2021936765

Printed in the United States of America

www.doceblant.com

This is based on actual events. Names, characters, places and incidents are the product of the author's imagination and used fictitiously. Any resemblance to actual persons, living or dead, including events and locations, is entirely coincidental.

Dear Seeker,

This book is for anyone who has an emotional, physical or spiritual issue. It's for the healer that wants a new and easy modality to help their clients. This book is for metaphysical teachers everywhere who would like a modality to pass on to their students that can be used every day with great success.

The manual you are holding in your hands contains the Healing and Regenerative Codes: stories, meditations, and important affirmative words to change your vibration. It contains channeling from the Holy Ones, my own Team of Light, guides, and guardians. We are all Holy Ones! Anyone can use this book as part of the course to become a healer or teacher of these codes; or simply read this book and use the information to raise your vibration! Best of luck to you!

The codes are a living, energy-infused image that enters the body's energetic field in a very specific way. The light codes can clear the mind of even the greatest over-thinker! The codes can be used all at once or individually and they can be directed in a cluster with intention for healing specific issues, such as grief and anxiety.

Many Blessings,

Mari Beckman

Table of Contents

Praise for *The Art of Your Energy* i

Chapter 1. The Art 1

Chapter 2. Channeling The Healing and Regenerative Codes 7

Chapter 3. Your Energetic Field 11

Chapter 4. Who Is The Healer? Who heals? 19

Chapter 5. The Gift you received on your birthday 23

Chapter 6. Listening to the body 27

Chapter 7. What is your body saying? 31

Chapter 8. Who are you, really? 33

Chapter 9. Overthinking and the Monkey Mind 37

Chapter 10. Hold your frequency 41

Chapter 11. Past Lives 47

Chapter 12. Awakening 53

Chapter 13. 5d and Beyond! Are We There Yet, Mom? 63

Chapter 14. Contact, the Real Disclosure 69

Chapter 15. Using The Codes 77

Thank you 113

Metaphysicians 115

CHAPTER 1:
The Art

Art communicates directly with your body as well as with your soul. If you have had the pleasure of holding a beautiful, sparkling amethyst in your hand and wonder at nature's magnificence, or to stand in front of a master's painting at a museum and feel the awe of creation, then you have felt art speaking to you!

Color arouses our emotions. How happy we are when we look outside on a perfect, sunny morning and see the first yellow daffodils greeting us! Or when we feel thrilled at the possibilities of a clear blue sky after rain, it's invigorating, peaceful and healing to our souls.

Your imagination, too, can help heal the body, mind and spirit. Healing the human body with energy work is like playing a video game. The more you use your imagination, the easier healing becomes.

As you read the first two paragraphs, were you able to see the violet amethyst in your mind's eye? The golden daffodils? If you could visualize them, you can easily learn to use the Healing and Regenerative Codes to heal yourself and others.

If you do not have the ability to visualize an image in your mind's eye, no matter. The Healing and Regenerative Codes will work anyway. There is not one issue written in this book that cannot be cleared by the codes. Everyone has access to their own higher skills, and by using the meditations and affirmations in this book and the codes, you will be able to heal yourself and learn to heal others.

This book is for anyone who has an emotional, physical or spiritual issue. It's for the healer that wants a new and easy modality to help their clients. This book is for metaphysical teachers everywhere who would like a modality to pass on to their students that can be used every day with great success. We have provided the work in both book and manual form.

The manual or book you are holding in your hands contains the Healing and Regenerative Codes; stories, meditations and important affirmative words to change your vibration. It contains channeling from the Holy Ones, my own Team of Light. One can use the manual as part of the course to become a healer or teacher of these codes; or simply read this book and use the information to raise your vibration! In fact, the book itself is a code that shifts human energy. Best of luck to you!

The Codes

The codes are a living, energy-infused image that enters the body's energetic field during a healing in a very specific way. The light codes can clear the mind of even the greatest over-thinker! The codes can be used all at once or individually and they can be directed in a cluster with intention for healing specific issues, such as grief and anxiety. During class, the codes are passed from teacher to student.

This original modality supports healing in the physical body, your mind, emotions and spirit. The system contains thirty-three codes that must be "boosted" energetically into the body of a client or student in a specific process. Anyone can learn this easy and powerful modality.

Imagine being able to clear old patterns and emotions that have weighed you down and even reduce and clear stubborn physical pain! Just like Reiki symbols, the Healing and Regenerative Codes, once boosted into the body of a student, will be available for use for the rest of your life and can be taught to others.

Jesus Christ:
"Use the codes joyfully, as they are given to you in the same spirit. Joy shall come if JOY is anticipated."

What is a Healing Light Code, Anyway?

As a healer and medium, I am regularly asked, when did I realize I "had a gift?" I always answer that I received my intuitive gifts on my birthday and so did you! We all did!

We are all intuitive and have the innate ability to heal ourselves and we can easily learn to heal others. As humans, we are nothing but light! We are multidimensional beings and as such, we are able to create and achieve more than what we might have been led to believe. We are limitless!

My Story; A Long, Strange Trip…

While working as a reader and healer, I have received many readings for myself at various venues and fairs. It's always fun to read for other psychics and receive readings as we hang out and catch up with one another. Many of my fellow readers have seen my past lives and it's the same story. It's always such fun to hear corroboration from my peers. When you find out the news of who you truly are, you will feel the truth of it in your heart! If you do not know the origin of your soul, ask a medium.

I am a Blue Ray Starseed and my soul origin is Angelic (Seraphim), Star (Arcturus and Sirius) and Stone. I have been here on Earth many lifetimes, but my soul originated with the Angels. My family is from the Holy Mother Mary line of Jesus Christ and the Ascended Master, Melchizedek. I have had a contract as a healer and a teacher in many lifetimes. I work only for Source and my religion is love. It doesn't sound as exciting to say that I now live in Tacoma, Washington with my husband and four dogs.

You will hear the words of many of my favorite guides in this book. These Spirit communications are a mix of the Holy Ones speaking directly to me or making a statement that is a universal one for all to hear. We all have the ability to understand communications from our guides and guardians in one way or another. So when you hear your guides and ancestors speak to you in symbols or numbers or if you hear angels whisper, don't just say "Who me?" We come from other realms, sit on galactic counsels and have agreed to be here now at the most exciting time during the great ascension of Earth. We find out our backstory to prove to us who we are and why we are here right now. Then it's time to move on, past ancient history, knowing we are powerful creator beings.

Ra:
"I come before you as a representative of the Galactic Federation of Light. There are many channels worldwide who speak with us as a group. We want you to understand that you have been a part of this collective for many lifetimes. Your contract as a healer is just that, a contract that exists in many worlds. Do not wonder if you understand your mission perfectly. You serve."

In my channeling over the last three years, I have heard my Team of Light speak of a new modality coming forth through me. Of course, I had no idea what they were talking about! Then, I was given the information that the regenerative, living light codes are in my DNA. They were implanted by me into my DNA in Lemuria. In other words, I took my work from that lifetime with me. I have since learned the way to release the codes out of me and into a client, student or teacher.

It Didn't Happen Overnight!

Since 2017, I thought I was writing a book! I was told to simply write and channel every day. I compiled stacks of notebooks full of hand-written channeling, observances and writings on all manner of metaphysical subjects and was told I would know when it was complete. So I wrote steadily for four years.

On a weekend in the summer of 2020, I was sitting in a Karuna® and Holy Fire Reiki® class and boom! I suddenly knew the book was not only a "book" at all! It is a book and a manual to a class, the very one you are reading right now.

That day my Companion Guide, through my higher self, showed me that the Healing and Regenerative Light Codes are inside me and, just like a Reiki attunement, light codes can be passed to a client, in a class either face-to-face or remotely, or to students who will then be able to teach the course and pass on the living codes to their students. The light codes are Angelic in origin and "held" by Archangel Metatron, the Seraphim, the Arcturians and the ascended masters, specifically Ascended Master Kuthumi.

The thirty-three codes will be anchored into the student's energetic field, in a transfer called a "boost". The student's frequency must be upgraded during the class over a two day period. Each of the thirty-three codes are designed to work with the human body, mind and spirit. Each of the codes does a specific job on their own or in combination and may be felt entering the energetic field. With this modality, the frequencies of the codes are "pulsed" into the student/client by the healer/instructor.

Saying Goodbye

Just prior to taking the Holy Fire® III Karuna Reiki® class, I made the decision to release all of my spirit guides and become a higher-self direct channel. It seemed as though I had a busload of guides! It was time for me to release all of them so that my abilities and frequency could rise higher, and the guides could go onto their next job. I'm sure I had exhausted a few of these incredible beings with my constant questions and "bad" food choices over the years! So the contracts were dissolved, and I spent what felt like months all alone. In reality, it was really only four weeks. I spoke only to the Creator and learned to better hear my own higher self. I'd been able to see and hear my own higher self and my client's higher selves but this was a brand-new game without the filter of my guidance team. I realized I could make the statement that when I speak with Beings of Light, I will only do so through my higher self. Then, one day, my favorite Companion Guide was back. I was so relieved and happy to see him! Before I stopped myself, I said, "Did you do what you needed to do?" He said he did! And within a few months, he told me of this modality. I could see it in an instant!

My Companion Guide

My Companion Guide and I have been together for many lifetimes. He was a great inventor and scientist. In one lifetime we were married. In this lifetime, we have worked together to birth the living light codes.

Once the codes were channeled and I learned to use them, I asked 22 people who were having physical, mental or emotional challenges to take part in a short trial. I sent the light codes daily for a week. I found that most people in the study felt relaxed and peaceful. Then I started a list of about 100 people with various issues and worked with them each day for months. The volunteers had a great variety of illnesses and concerns ranging from cancer to shingles to depression. This was the beginning and today I use the codes in every healing, with every client. I use them on myself every day.

> ***Companion Guide:***
> *"You are moving into a new corridor. You are rising into higher dimensions for your healing purposes as well as ascending along with the rest of humanity. Your regenerative codes have assisted you to rise out of the 12th dimension. As of today, you have attained a much higher frequency. Go ahead and play with this new energy. The codes are passed as we showed you through Archangel Metatron and me, along with others, including Angels and Ascended Masters that assist with this new modality."*
>
> *"This weekend was a test for all. The energy of the planetary alignments and the frequency patterning will continue to adjust each human. Any wondering about how to change now is moot as the change is currently happening to all on Earth. Early January 2020 was the blast off, an opening; now all will be revealed. Good work from all of you, without worry, is required. The outcome is unknown as it has not been created yet. A reboot is an old way of seeing the issue. A new look is what is required*

going forward. Need to know causes anxiety. You shall remember, and continue to remember and in this pattern, life is revealed."

Commander Ashtar:
"You are now activated in all 12 chakras for transmission of light codes. These are your light activations that have come with you through your own DNA strands. This frequency will increase as you work with more people."

CHAPTER 2:
Channeling The Healing and Regenerative Codes

Every healer differs within their skill level and mode of practice. When a healer learns a new skill and practices that skill over and over on herself and her clients, she is bound to make the modality her own during readings and healings. Some healers see symbols in a client's energetic field. I also work with everyday symbols that I see in my client's energy field. All the information that is needed for a reading or healing is in the energetic field and it is laid out like a map or a living tarot spread. When I work with a client, I ask for only their birthday and always begin the session with an energetic clearing, regardless of why the sitter (client) has come to see me. Once cleared, the energetic field shows me the answers to most questions, or the sitter's guides or higher self will speak to any question.

My healing practice evolved from learning Usui Reiki and becoming a Reiki Master in 2003, then learning Quantum Touch in 2005 and teaching myself my own various modalities given to me through my guides. I taught myself The Emotion Code and Matrix Energetics, though I am not certified in either of the last two techniques. I do my own version of both, rolling in emotional release and heart and brain entrainment as my guides have taught me. I am also a Master in Holy Fire® III Karuna Reiki®.

The Healing and Regenerative Codes were channeled in five at a time over a one-month period. Once we had all of them, my husband, Thom Beckman, and I worked on them over and over again with guidance until the final set of thirty-three were complete. Adding in the directions and "powering up" the codes took another month. During this time I, too, powered up. Learning the best way to use the codes evolved over time with help from the volunteer's input and guidance from my Spirit Team. Learning to use the "boost and tap" features came near the end. Then, I learned how to pass the codes to students and teachers.

Energy Never Lies

Symbols or markers in the energetic field show up in a healing, like a little roadmap to follow. Guidance and higher selves show me what needs to be cleared first in every healing. The healing starts and ends from A-to-Z and I follow the everyday symbols like a path. The higher self of the client chooses a template or a movie for me to follow. We start with grounding and aligning and then progress as the higher self of the client and their guidance directs. Often there is much to do and so I ask my client to only speak when asked a question directly and then simply answer yes or no so that the session unfolds as their higher self-wishes. Of course, near the end of the session, clients can ask questions.

Every Day and Universal Symbols In the Energetic Field

Symbols are fascinating! Even if I do not know what the symbol means right away, and occasionally that happens as symbols can be endless; generally the client will understand what the symbol means. Clearing happens in a variety of ways. It's inspirational to watch the symbols come up and then change as clearing and healing unfold. I might see crystals, colors, flowers, birds, geometric shapes or numbers that all point out what needs to happen next, in order to advance healing. If a healer sees an aardvark and doesn't understand what it is, don't worry or discount it! That aardvark is there for a reason! Trust and ask it why it has shown up. If I can't figure out why I see a symbol, or if it's an unfamiliar one, I just ask the sitter's higher self or guidance team what the symbol means.

Sample Symbols

Most healers have their "own" symbols and others are universal. Color can be a code and each color means something specific.

Color in Healing

Color has long been used in healing. I wait until the client's higher self shows me a color before running it through the body. Emerald green for healing and harmony, pink for relaxation or release, and so on.

I can determine when certain guides or hierarchy come in during a meditation or healing by the colors they show me. For example, blue for the Angels, pink for the Holy Mother Mary, rainbow for the unicorns and so on. There are some colors that are seen and accepted worldwide but I would add, most folks see what they see. We all see patterns and color differently. In the condition called synesthesia, people report being able to smell colors or hear numbers. Everyone is completely different. So bear this in mind when working with color.

The higher self or guidance team will illuminate areas in the body and energetic field to work on in a healing session by lighting them up in different colors. Sometimes the colors are meant to be held or moved through that area, for example, emerald green in the stomach area. Sometimes, color will show an imbalance. Of course, each healer may use color in a different way.

A few symbols I regularly see in a session:

- Hands stuck together
- Feet in a hole or feet in the earth
- Grey mist over head
- Numbers
- Animals and birds
- Geometric shapes
- Arrows pointing the way
- Many, many others

The Healing and Regenerative Codes Used Within a Session

The Healing and Regenerative codes are added to the client's energetic field to heal body, mind and spirit. These codes are light language. The codes can be added at any time during a healing and are usually added several times during the healing depending on what is to be cleared.

What is Light Language?

Light language is a communication from Source through human voice or art. Each artist interprets their light language in their own unique way. Light language can be sung, toned, spoken, drawn, painted or visually transferred through hand or body movement.

Approximately a year prior to receiving the light codes, I began to notice symbols and colors, almost like a mist outside of my body or the client's body. I realized the colors and symbols were meant to enter the energetic field. This was the beginning of the healing and regenerative codes. As all beautiful work that unfolds through Spirit, it was all in timing. I had to be able to hold the energy of the codes and learn to use them. A template or path to healing shows up during each session. Symbols and colors showing up in the template may also indicate that the healer's frequency has been adjusted. Pay close attention to the template spirit gives you as it changes as your frequency changes. The template also may change according to the time of year and the client's needs.

How are the Healing and Regenerative Codes Used?

The codes are a living light language. All thirty-three codes can be placed in the body during a healing, either at one time or in a sequence, called a "stream". The healer or teacher can also use the codes individually or in combination to clear the body, mind and spirit. During the initial opening of the student's energy to the new modality, the codes are boosted in. Once the regenerative codes are entered into the energy field of the student, they remain a part of the student forever. The light codes can then be used in person during a healing or sent remotely. Once the intention to send the codes has been stated by the healer, the template is put forth in a specific manner by the higher self of the client and the codes are held in the mind and sent through the heart field. The student or client may be able to see or feel the codes entering the energetic field depending on the way in which they perceive energy. Immediately, the frequency of the student or client is upgraded, and a sense of peace is felt.

> *Master Acupuncturist:*
> "The purpose of the healer is to show up and light up the possibilities in a person who is ill or struggling. Our purpose as healer is to challenge the client and always to love. Love is the greatest healer any of us have ever known. So be sure, every time with each case, and each individual, whether human or animal, we honor and love them. Then, only then, have you done your job."

> *Nostradamus:*
> "The human energy field, together and all working in concert, can be the breaker of lower frequencies. Use your voice to disseminate this reality for some do not know. Now is not the time to go small with fear."

CHAPTER 3:

Your Energetic Field

There is a field of energy (aura) around every living person, animal, tree and plant. Even inanimate objects have an energy field. This has been proven by Kirlian photography whereby the energetic field can be seen in photos. This energetic field connects humans to all living things and to each other! Healers who use the pendulum can demonstrate changes in a client's energetic field before and after a healing session. Energetic changes can be felt through the hands of a healer.

Your energetic field can be glowing bright and lit up all around you like a Christmas tree or it can be gray and muddled, depending on your emotional health. Aura colors constantly change with emotions.

The chakra system is a part of your energetic field. Most people are aware of the seven major chakras; root, sacral, solar plexus, heart, throat, third eye, and crown. There are also five additional major chakras: Earth Star, below your feet and soul star, spirit, universal, galactic, and stellar gateway, above the head. There are many small chakras in your hands, feet and face called nadi, as well as chakra antennae around your head. These 12 major chakras run through the central column of the body and connect us to the Sun and into the center of the Earth.

Chakras have a color, a tone, a spin and their own vibrational frequency. Data is stored in each chakra and when cleared, the body, mind and spirit will return to flow. Your auric field changes constantly depending upon the intensity of your chakra's energy and the auric field will show that chakra's predominant color. A human's energy field is a beautiful work of art! In fact, I believe the rainbow bridge is the chakra system. When nearing death, the chakras dim and the rainbow bridge appears. This is an image I've seen many times when people and pets pass away.

We as human beings can feel each other's emotions to varying degrees. Clearing, strengthening and armoring our own energetic field allows us to be in the presence of others and take on a smaller dose of their emotional energy. It is so important to have a clearing and armoring system set up to do each day. Each morning when I wake up I drink a glass of water and call into unity my body, mind and spirit. After a night of sleep and astral travel, it is important to command ourselves to reunify. When we lovingly command reunification, we are calling in our body, mind, spirit (soul), aspects of ourselves, higher self and inner child back into unity.

Daily Reunification Commands for Energetic Integrity

- "I call in the highest frequency I can attain each day, in ease."
  (We must add the words "in ease" so we will not struggle all day if the overriding frequency is high and we are in a lower energetic frequency.)

- "I call in the golden sunlight from the seven Galactic Suns through our own portal Sun and in and through our physical body and down into the core of Earth itself. I visualize my grounding cords falling out from my foot chakra portals and winding down into the core. I tightly wrap my grounding cords around the blue crystal core of Earth. I raise my consciousness up from the core of the Earth and find myself standing back at the template."

- The day's template will come from my higher self. It may be the ocean, a river, a desert or forest. It can be a place I have visited or a place I do not recognize from this lifetime. The template may not be on this Earth. Trust and have faith in your practices. Do these practices every morning and again during the day. Use a guided meditation if your brain is busy.

I Expect Good Things to Happen Mantra:

- I am constantly thriving in the frequency of love and acceptance and in the easy flow of energy.

- So therefore, I expect kind and loving treatment from others.

- I expect to stay in abundance, and I call in the abundance that was always meant for me. No matter why I didn't receive this abundance earlier, I welcome it now.

- I allow for differences in others' beliefs and opinions and therefore, I hold those people in my life, who see things differently than I do, in love. I allow myself to change my mind even if I've learned beliefs and opinions from my family or early learning.

- I expect to assist others in a 50-50 manner, so therefore I expect that others will assist me when I need them to help me in some way.

- If I have assisted others by sending my own Teams of Light, I call them back to me. I call back the Angels that support me, including my Guardian Angel. If I pray for others, I call in their Angels and Teams of Light.

Meditation: How Do You Do It?

People say their brain just will not quiet down enough to meditate. That is the best reason to start meditating! Even after a good 25 years of meditation, sometimes my mind drifts. No problem. Just begin again. Start out learning to meditate with a spoken meditation from a YouTube recording of a voice that resonates with you. A peaceful voice over beautiful music is a great way to begin. Twenty minutes of meditation each day can change your life. It's better than sleep! It's the perfect way to begin or end your day.

Holy Mother Mary:
"Bring your problems to me. Leave them at my feet."

Committing to anything new takes intention and a really good statement. Intend to commit to a month of daily meditation. Say your goal out loud. You do not have to find a perfect spot or a perfect crystal. Just sit in your own comfortable chair with your feet on the ground. Find a meditation that suits your purpose, such as chakra clearing or relaxation.

Meditation releases the brain chemical oxytocin, the love hormone. Sitting up is a great way to start out because then you have a good chance of not falling asleep. If you do, the meditation time is not lost. The information still gets into the brain and body.

I believe sitting in meditation every day gets you ready to consciously journey with your Team of Light. Soon you will notice that there is something going on in your mind while you meditate! Maybe you begin to see a path or the ocean or a beautiful mountain. When I meditate or work with clients, Spirit gives me a template. This template can be by the ocean, in a desert, on a mountain or off world. Next time the template may change depending on what needs to get done during the healing. The path within the template may be made of golden bricks or made of crystal; emerald green for focused healing or amethyst for bringing in self-love. Maybe the path is golden citrine to raise your energy. Pay close attention to your own movie in your mind!

A Visit to Nirvana Meditation:

- I focus on my breath as I relax. As I take in my breath through my nose, my lower belly rises up, and as I exhale, my breath comes out my nose. In a moment, I breathe easily.

- I lovingly command my endorphins to release.

- I intend that any pain I am experiencing simply fades away.

- I am speaking directly to my muscles. My muscles relax and release easily and completely.

- I relax into the peace and beyond peace is where I find myself.

- As I flow into peace, I imagine a beautiful garden. I noticed lush, green grass, flowers and blooming trees.

- I am in my own heaven, where all is possible.

- I see row after row of tables laden with cups of sparkling, fresh water.

- I see my beloved deceased before me, I am so happy! I am here for a relaxing visit.

- As I walk past the tables, there are familiar faces and some people I do not know; they are the faces of my ancestors.
- I see my beloved pets that have crossed over.
- They are all so happy to see me! I thank them for coming here to meet me.
- I sit with my family in this beautiful place for a while. I take a good rest.
- When I am rested, I thank everyone for coming, and I walk back the way I came in earlier, watching my bare feet on the vibrant green grass.
- I find myself at the front door of my home.
- I return to my body refreshed.

How Do You Awaken Kundalini?

Kundalini can be awakened through meditation and yoga. It is the source of chi or prana at the base of your spine that rises up through the central channel. It is a beautiful clearing and activation that can come on suddenly. Make the intention that you are ready to awaken kundalini.

Sit up straight for meditation.

- Focus your breath and breathe from root to crown.
- Listen to music or binaural beats.
- Be patient with yourself.
- Intend to experience kundalini.
- Chant or tone the Bija mantras or your favorite chant.

The Bija or seed mantras resonate, each at a different frequency, and when toned or chanted clear their specific chakra. This assists in the flow of chi (prana, energy) to balance the chakras and encourage the opening of kundalini.

The Bija Mantras:

Root Chakra - Red - Lam

Sacral - Orange - Vam

Solar Plexus - Yellow - Ram

Heart - Green - Yam

Throat - Blue - Ham

Third Eye - Indigo - Om

Crown - Violet - Om

Healing the Body

Companion Guide:
"Find love in the speedy motion of alignment and all healing. Love is the grease that clears every stuck wheel."

Your body is designed to easily heal and reflect strength and stamina. Good health is a human birthright. As humans, we hold an innate intelligence that runs the body's systems effortlessly and without any conscious thought. Have you really ever thought about your liver or esophagus if you didn't have to? And yet there it is, doing a great job for you all day long! Have you ever wondered why some people can quickly heal after an accident or medical procedure and some folks seem to never heal or only go just so far in the healing process?

There are many reasons the body is resistant or slow in healing. We must keep in mind that some accidents and illnesses are written into a person's life by the needs of their own soul for growth. As we all can testify, sometimes being laid up brings us clarity and lessons along with healing and rest. But sometimes a broken ankle is just a broken ankle!

This is the prime reason to pay attention to your body. It always wants to speak to us! After a period of time of not paying attention to the body, the body will send a few quiet signals. If you miss those, it will literally scream "Listen to me!" or "You are not paying attention!" Pain, illness, broken bones and falls all can be communication.

When I tune into my client's body and organs, I can often see and feel distress. Diet, rest, meditation, exercise and holistic therapies can be added at any time along with Western medicine, if needed; and it can make a tremendous difference in how the body heals.

The Lesson of Pain

Remember, we do not need to be busy all day to be productive. Each day rest a bit and recuperate when you need to. Do all you can to support your body while it heals.

The lesson of pain and stillness is available for all of us to learn each time an illness, accident or trauma comes along. Don't wait for surgery or to be laid up in traction! Ask your body early on. Each illness is a perfect time to go within and ask yourself; has this happened before? Is this illness a pattern for me? Why do I continue to have stomach or back issues, etc.? Why is this illness coming back?

Just like everyone, the body wishes to be respected and heard. Life goes so fast that we sometimes forget to eat right during busy or stressful times and sleep can become elusive. Sometimes there isn't time made for exercise. So then the body may speak up with all types of distress calls such as pain and malfunction. Believe what your body is saying when it tells you it hurts! Constant mind chatter, blocking and resisting won't help at all, it just makes it harder to clear illness, pain and disease. Releasing and reunifying meditations work wonders to begin your day. Get used to a daily practice so you can hear your body speak to you. It is not the time during a crisis to be hard on yourself for being ill. Just listen closely to what the body wants to say.

Nostradamus:
"Why did it have to be so hard? My dear, you know full well it isn't easy to release all the emotions, ones that have been with you for decades. Everyone is going through it! Some folks are so much more resistant than others. Remember, when you have had memories come up that surprised you but then you allowed them to surface? Having resistance causes such tension in the physical body. Physical pain and illness can be a result. Sometimes this happens over and over again. The human resists going deep into their own darkness and yet, the energy right now requires it. Remember, the sweet release you had when you wrote about those surfacing memories and spoke about them? You will continue to release them. So keep going! There are more. Your mental health was served by looking away. You survived and now you are safe to take a long, deep look inside yourself."

Cording and Family Patterns

An etheric cord, or energetic attachment, can occur between two people and can be a positive experience or a difficult one. A cord can be a beautiful connection between lovers and friends, or it can be a draining experience if one person is needy or controlling and seeks to suck energy from the person they are corded with.

The cord allows us to feel a close connection. When you feel it's time to sever this connection, bring your focus to your solar plexus or wherever the cord is attached, and intend to feel the cord. Pull it out by the root. I imagine it like a big yellow onion! Pulling the cord out tends to work better than cutting it. Intend that the cord returns to Earth.

Archangel Michael:
"Cording is useful. One learns to feel emotions this way. If a cord is present, it is time to take a proper look at why this happens."

Seven-Generational Release, Inspired by Jenny Grace (Run this energetic release three times.):

- I call in my beloved ancestors. I honor you and thank you. My wish is to release and integrate the energy that holds me to addiction, illness, choices, emotions, family patterns or programming that keeps me from being free.

- I call on the generations that have come before me back to the beginning of time. I ask that you stand with me as I release and integrate this energy back to zero point.

- I call in the seven generations that come after me, present with all my aspects from parallel lifetimes from all worlds. I ask that you stand with me as I release and integrate the energy that binds us. Energy never dissipates, if you do not wish to take part in the ceremony now, know that you can at the time of your choosing.

- I release what holds us in bondage, fore and aft, and I ask that I receive a symbol that this work has completed.

Healer Derek Condit:
"I revoke any dream state agreements that are not in alignment with my higher self, and I fill the space left with love."

Armoring Technique Taught by Derek Condit, Intuitive/Clairvoyant, Energy Healer and Owner of Mystical Wares

- I light up my heart space.
- I flow the diamond light into my chest and then into my body.
- I flow the light into my head and extremities.
- I bring the light into my home.
- I configure a soccer ball shape around my own energetic field, painting it with silver mirror paint, inside and out.

I do the armoring technique every day along with other visualizations. Say these words every day and then make the intention known to your guides and energetic field that when you say the word "armoring" or visualize a particular color that means armoring, you are immediately armored.

We get busy, so intend to have a few tricks up your sleeve regarding armoring and clearing your energy. Once or twice each day say the entire intention, then armor throughout the day by using the color or the word. Same thing with clearing, intend to have many levels. A big clearing in the morning and in the evening along with some quick clearings during the day. This way, you can easily and quickly clear and armor yourself between daily interactions with people or working with a client.

Imagination, Dialogue and Intention

I begin each day by saying the Reunification Commands for Energetic Integrity (see Chapter 3) first thing in the morning. Then I speak out loud a list of all the things that I am grateful for. The list of what I'm grateful for changes, but it might sound like:

"Holy Ones! (We are all holy ones, I am speaking to Creator God, my Team of Light, my body, aspects of me, higher self and guidance team) I am so grateful for my life! Thank you for my husband, my friends, crystals, the dogs and the beautiful day."

I start out the day with a big glass of water and my supplements. I fast for at least 12 to 16 hours overnight after my last meal so that my body and organs have a rest. I am vegetarian for my own health. This works for my body. I believe every person's body will ask for what it needs. Sometimes I eat with intuition. When the body requires grounding, I may add other items. No one's diet is right for everyone and often it takes time to find what food and drinks trigger our body to feel discomfort.

I then ask if my body requires energy work. I visualize my ship of light or Merkaba around me. The Merkaba's sacred geometric shape is the star tetrahedron. The daily work may be tapping, toning, light coding or listening to a favorite meditation teacher on YouTube. I use the Bija Mantras to clear my chakras and I run Holy Fire Reiki. Each day's energy work may be different than the day before depending on what the body wants.

Try these daily practices or use your own. Any daily practice that you are willing to do becomes a ritual that you'll look forward to and won't want to miss. This practice opens the path to healing.

Chapter 4:

Who Is The Healer? Who heals?

Are you ready to commit to change? Are you ready to change your diet, add an exercise routine, or completely change your attitude towards healing? What about changing your lifestyle to begin to focus on health? Can you forgive yourself and others? Have you learned the lesson your illness brought to you?

If you answered yes, your vibrational state will continue to rise and change with the good decisions you are ready to make when you commit to health every day. Health and healing must be your top priority. Stasis limits all growth! Sometimes it is a series of small blockages on the way to your return back to health. The small blocks or stops can simply be the need to change a routine. All life is a ritual as Merlin the Alchemist said, and your daily habits certainly can create either stuckness, blockage or flow. Making time for healthy daily rituals and practices is imperative for healing and maintaining your own good health.

Start with a few new guidelines or changes. Make a vow that every day you will do a bit of exercise. Go outside, if you can, for a walk. Start out slow. Regular changes that you adhere to each day becomes healthy habits or the ritual that you look forward to. Subtract all unhealthy food and drink from your diet. Even if you do this in stages, it will be beneficial.

The Ritual of Healing

Ultimately, a question you can ask yourself is: does my diet and lifestyle support my body, mind and spirit? If the answer is no, only you can find the food choices that nourish you completely.

But can you stick to it for the long-haul? Only you can answer that. People love to judge each other about diet. There is no better diet than the one that brings health and well-being and that you'll stick to because it makes you feel great!

Also, be sure you are not overly hungry. I found that when I stretch my fast to 12 to 15 hours, I was not hungry at all. This was helpful to give my body extended time to rest and process. So if I have dinner at 7:00 p.m., I do not eat again until at least 10:00 a.m. or later. Please research intermittent fasting before you start this type of program. Water or juice fasting can be beneficial to health. There are many books available on fasting and of course, it is always best to speak with your naturopath or holistic doctor first, in order to get all the information you need when making big changes in your diet.

The most important part of changing my diet came to me in a way I hadn't anticipated. In the past, I would spend all day feeling down about what I was eating. Way too much sugar (for years!) had held me hostage to the belief that sugar would lift my spirits, give me energy and the push to be able to accomplish more during the day. That is the lie that sugar tells us! Are you a person that can eat a small piece of candy and not eat another sweet treat until next week? Yes, I know people like you are out there! I am not that person and never have been. If that big, beautiful box of candy is in front of me I'm going to eat quite a bit of it! And finish it the next day. But I recognized that eating that way harmed me and caused me to overthink about what I was eating constantly. It's a loop! It is easier to not eat sugar at all. So, over the years, I have had many swaths of time where I am sugar-free. Looking back, those are my best days. Not only because the body feels better, with less pain, fatigue and wonky blood sugar, but my mental health does not suffer with me constantly blaming myself for choices I made during the day.

I found that the supplement Gemnema has helped tremendously in releasing my sugar habit.

As always, ask your favorite holistic practitioner for the okay to add in any supplements. Sugar is a drug. Giving it up can be a huge part of healing.

Forgiving ourselves for what brought us to this point is most important. Have you gone through a difficult time in your life and reacted with overeating? All may be ready to be released to begin again with a clean slate. Forgive those people who took part in your illness because maybe that alliance, with all its hardship, was part of a soul contract. Recognize this, trust and practice forgiveness.

The Body Speaks

Albert Einstein:
"The biofield is the only reality."

Jesus Christ:
"Now is the time for self-care. Freedom is in the doing and not in the thinking."

It's certainly a challenge for us humans to eat to live, rather than to live to eat. We can be hung up on the thought that it is the only pleasure left to us. We may feel as though we gave everything else up! However, a varied and healthful diet with lots of fresh water provides the platform for true healing.

This manual contains writing and channeling from notebooks I kept for over a four year period. Re-reading through all of my notebooks was eye-opening. Many times Spirit revealed that I was ready to bring in a healing technique that is brand new. The loving messages I received were a mix of channeling for others, the planet and myself. I received many lovely (and pointed!) messages about the care and feeding of my own body.

The channeling regarding the new and unknown information was not something I recognized. I did not concern myself with what exactly it was. I believe wholeheartedly that when the timing is right, Spirit would show up. I would be ready because my intention is in place to work together with my Team of Light and higher self in Divine timing and with Divine will.

Why did it take so long to change my eating habits and take better care of myself? Why do I sometimes fall off the wagon? Probably all the same reasons that anyone else holds onto before a big change! I made changes but some didn't stick. How long does it take us to change a habit? I believe it is different for everyone.

The Lies I Told Myself About Food:

- Chocolate is the only vice I have left.
- I'm too tired to go for a walk, I'll just eat less today.
- I'll just eat the unhealthy food I have in my refrigerator and cabinets before I switch back to being a healthier eater.

Eating and Drinking with Joy

Over and over my Team of Light reminded me how my body feels when I eat correctly and incorrectly. I must decide, they said, if I am willing to love myself so much that I will pay attention to what I'm eating. I must cook healthy meals and drink adequate nourishing fluids and support my nutrition with the right supplements and vitamins, and on and on.

I was a vegetarian for five years and loved it. For some of those years I did not use balanced supplements and food combinations and my health declined. I now had to be ready to focus on what my entire system was requesting.

> *Gilgamesh the Warrior:*
> *"Many of you are still disconnected from what truly can bring your health back into balance. As long as one looks outside of oneself for healing, true health can never be completely attained. Food that is alive and healthy, prepared as a little as possible and consumed with life-giving water, will bring full circle healing. Any program of eating that does not cut out processed food, sugar and chemical additives will not be a supportive diet. Do not eat poison. We don't mean to keep you from satisfying a sweet craving or celebrating a special time with food. But we need to admonish you to keep a clean diet for the better part of your day. Most do not drink enough water to support the body and brain. Once the optimum water level is reached and continued, the body's energy will rise and even sleep will normalize. Headaches, and stress on the brain will be reduced. Human bodies have become resistant to the onslaught of chemicals in food on the planet. Many diseases can be healed with proper food and a new diet. The light, the very life, has been extinguished from your food. Make your choices well to bring back health."*

I add three shungite nuggets to my water pitcher. Shungite, a carbon-based mineral from Karelia, Russia, purifies the water and eliminates toxins. By placing three nuggets together in your water container, a coherent field is created that clears the water of contaminates.

I also intend that the water I drink is high-quality and will match or lift my frequency.

Dr. Masaru Emoto wrote, "*Just before we drink water, say: 'Thank you. I love you.'* Say these words out loud or in your heart, because water receives the hado or vibration that you emit."

This practice uplifts and aligns the water with your body. We also should thank the beautiful lakes, rivers and oceans of the world for all they do! Water is so important, after all our bodies are made up of roughly 60% to 70% water, depending on gender and weight.

Giving thanks before eating a meal is a familiar part of the day for people all over the world. But have you really thought of what energy you are placing into the nutritious (or not) food you are about to take into your body? As you pray over it, value your meal, honor it. Intend that it is not taken for granted. Revitalize the food with high frequency, amp it up! Thank your food and be grateful.

For a year, I chose chlorella to detoxify my system along other supplements. I had the amalgam fillings in my teeth removed. I supported my body with meat for a very short time before returning to a 95% vegetarian lifestyle. I now pay attention to what my own body says it wants each day.

I am including my own testimony to show that the body never stops communicating if it is unhealthy and unhappy. Listen and learn what your body is trying desperately to say. For this, we must understand what higher skills you have available to use right now. And, most importantly, you must be ready and willing, as well as energetically open and receptive, to making these changes to improve your own life.

If you decide to make changes for better health, your outward appearance shall reflect it. Your challenge is to accept the changes with a happy heart and notice how people react to you in a positive manner. This will stimulate you to accomplish even more! Do not be afraid of changes in your outward appearance. Your wardrobe, your makeup, your hair and your energy, above all, will continue to adjust with your ongoing focus on healing.

CHAPTER 5:
The Gift you received on your birthday

Remember, everyone is intuitive. If we focus on the skills we have innately, we can become psychic. Usually, people have one or two higher skills that they use the most to understand the unseen world around them. Many "sensitives" have all the "claires", clairvoyance, clairaudience, clairsentience and so on.

To have a clear vision of the future, one is known as a clairvoyant. Everyone can understand that once in a while we have flashes of knowledge that may not make any sense at all. Some call it gut instinct, the shine, "spidey sense," or mojo. Personal magic! Clairvoyants have a great spatial awareness! We are good daydreamers. Once we have a few visions come true, it's easier to trust your gut.

Clairaudience or clear hearing happens in two distinct ways. Inside the mind, a voice (yours usually) will pipe up with a command such as "Slow down!" if you are driving too fast or working too hard. This can be your guardian angel speaking right next to you in the passenger seat! It can be the voice of a loved one on the other side or even a voice outside your head. Recently, I heard "Take off your headphones!" from a guide. Of course, there is always the story of hearing one's name called. Remember, the deceased and your guides will bend over backwards to communicate with you!

Claircognizance is clear knowing. You just know that you know something. This skill is particularly great to have while dating! Or in business! It can save you heartache and time. People flock to you; they love to tell you their problems. Folks with the skill are very sensitive to large groups of people. You may be an empath and be able to feel others' emotions as if they were your own. Being an empath is a superpower! There are so many ways to understand and work with this special skill without it running you.

Clairsentience is the skill one uses in psychometry or the ability to get information by touching an object. It also is the skill of picking up energy in a building.

Clairolfaction is the name for the higher sense of smell and clairgustance, clear taste. These skills and more are available to the sensitive person. Smelling your deceased grandmother's perfume or a particular spice your mother used in cooking or tasting something bitter can be a clue to who may be coming through for a visit from the other side.

I Declare (an affirmation)

- It's a beautiful morning!
- I declare that today will be a peaceful day.
- I prefer peace; therefore I choose to focus on peace today.
- I actively listen to that voice inside me that keeps me safe all day. I am aware and safe.
- I get things done! My established routine of ease and flow makes the day fly by, as I make good progress getting through my tasks.
- I raise my frequency so that I may access my higher skills.

Become your own healer. It's the power position one can stand in to call back good health. All you need is imagination, dialogue and intention. See your goal happening right in front of you! It is the perfect chance to do some daydreaming which can help you tune into the higher realms.

What is your goal for healing yourself? Are you looking for pain relief, functionality or better range of motion? Are you ready to get off medication including the over-the-counter types? Goal setting can help.

The intention to heal is important. Sometimes we feel like we are beaten down by pain and disability. We can't see our goal easily or we have tried so many modalities and therapies or healers, that we just give up on manifesting better health.

You will notice that as you awaken, manifestation becomes even easier to do. I love manifesting! Writing down monthly and yearly goals can be a game changer. Get a whiteboard or a special notebook so you can look back on what you listed. It's always fun to do it on New Year's Eve! I keep a box of readings that people do for me along with business cards or memories of what I did for the year. On New Year's Eve, I turn it upside down on the kitchen counter to see what the year held. You can include your own manifestations in your yearly box and they may look something like this:

I find the perfect home for me. It includes…

- My healing goals for this month are…
- I limit screen time to…
- I walk every day.
- I easily make friends.
- Money is just energy. I flow that energy towards me.
- I live within my means.

There are extra special days throughout the year that are great for manifesting. The double-digit power number of January 11 or February 22 or special days such as Solstice or Fall Equinox. Or any day that has special meaning for you is auspicious.

Goals keep us on track. A month's worth of goals met, become habits we stick to and use to structure our days and nights. Bring in those manifestations clearly, whisk them along on an emotion such as love, joy and optimism. Now stop thinking about it! The universe has heard you.

As for habits, the goal, of course, is to create positive ones. But, most people have habits they wish they could release. The Healing and Regenerative Light Codes do a great job in assisting people to clear all manner of habits easily.

CHAPTER 6:

Listening to the body

There are tools to use to help tune into your body. An easy way to understand what the body wishes to tell you, is to use a pendulum. In fact, your own body can be the pendulum.

How Does Pendulum Dowsing Work?

A pendulum has been used to find minerals, water, lost items, lost people and answer all manner of questions for hundreds of years.

The pendulum was my first metaphysical tool. It's really my only tool, other than crystals and my healing energy wands. Intention and mutual attraction go hand-in-hand with choosing a pendulum. The first question to ask when you are ready to buy one is "Will you work with me?"

You may be attracted to a lovely amethyst or hematite crystal pendulum but when you ask if it likes you… nope, won't move. It's not yours. Go to a metaphysical store where you can touch lots of pendulums. Find the one that seems the most energetic in your hand and feels just right.

My favorite one is a little copper pendulum. Not too heavy for work but solid and strong enough to receive a sharp answer. I'll ask yes/no questions to start and then once I purchase a new pendulum, I program it to work for me. It's a working contract.

Say these words out loud to your pendulum or body:

- Answers will come from my higher self, a client's higher self, or our Team of Light.

- Pendulum will show percentages, emotional frequency, and physical health and more.

- My body is a pendulum. (I rock forward for yes and backwards for no.) Your body sign may be different.

The pendulum will work differently for each seeker. Don't get discouraged if the pendulum swing is small or slow in the beginning. As you become acquainted, the energy will bloom. Make sure it moves when you ask a question. Go through quite a few pendulums until you find the one you love that loves you back and will work with you and your higher self. I keep a dish in several areas of my home to hold my pendulum so it's always in easy reach. I place it on selenite or citrine to regularly clear it.

Who are You, Really?

The release of who we once were is imperative. Right now is the truest time of new beginnings. Even if you just learned you were the King of Siam in a past life, celebrate yourself! It's cool to be king but bring yourself back to this moment right now. When we release past life associations, all old allegiances, timelines, structures and even families, we bring our self into this now. It is a freedom to just be you.

We humans are beautiful multi-dimensional beings of light. Each of us has an inner child within us, along with our soul and higher self. We all have aspects from other dimensions within us and we all belong to a soul monad or oversoul that holds 144 souls. We have a system of chakras with a body full of cells that hear every word we speak and believe everything we say. Just a simple speaking up that YOU are sovereign and a creator being with a valid voice is a beautiful beginning! State that you are ready to hear your guides speak through your higher self and that your own higher self or authentic self is in first position now. Get ready to change your reality! We are directors of our own healing and when we recognize this fact and bring all of our fractals back together, we are on our way to becoming whole and well. It is like bringing the accordion back together. This is the return to embodiment, and it is the process of uniting all of our human original structure and the energetic system returning to its own zero point. Zero point is the essence or the beginning of all creation. When I have done embodiment ceremonies in class, people have explained that the sensation of reuniting feels like a peacock releasing its feathers or like suddenly developing extra arms. It's a different experience for each person.

> *Archangel Gabriel:*
> *"Each person has his or her own soul's destiny. No one comes to this Earth plane without a clearly set out blueprint of what their life will be. From the family one chooses, to your life's work, your guides have poured over your soul's choices along with you. No one thing is left out; everything that happens is a thought-out process. The soul's enlightenment is priority. Many souls weigh in; your guides and masters and your very own soul makes the choice as to where and when it reincarnates. This happens when the time is right. God has made just enough souls. There has never been a time when God wasn't in control of each soul's destiny."*

Your Inner Child

> *Holy Mother Mary:*
> *"I am here, of course I am! Always. I am you and you are me. Gratitude is the key and the human heart, the lock. But 'I AM that I AM' is the link between God and child. How do you feel when you hear a certain song? Longing, pain, happiness, the bliss you felt when I came before you years ago? Your awakening continues to this day."*

You have an inner child within you that is creative and innocent, pure and fun loving. She is also the true record of painful childhood memories, emotions and trauma that was a part of your life before puberty. When we take part in a soul retrieval or learn to do inner child work, we speak directly to this very real part of our subconscious.

Inner child recall and soul retrieval exercises can be accomplished through a beautiful meditative journey or ceremony or done within a healing session.

The way I begin the exercise is to have the client repeat three phrases at the appropriate time within their healing. After the three sentences are repeated, the client will usually feel an emotional or physical release. At that point, the inner child will show us the ages when trauma occurred, and we will continue to call back the soul fragments with other welcoming words determined by what the higher self puts forth. Most likely, the client will also experience some type of sensation either in the body or experience an emotional release. I was taught this process and made it my own. I invite you to do the same. This process is used by many healers.

The Retrieval:
- "My inner child, I invite you to come back together with my higher self.
- I invite all inner children that I've ever been into this healing.
- I call back to me all unhealed fragments of my soul from any lifetime I've ever lived."

Multidimensional You

Our soul is part of the eternal Divine. It's who we are without a body! The soul contains all aspects of ourselves and cares for our inner child. The term higher or highest self refers to our eternal, awakened self. When we are ready to speak to our guidance team through our higher self, it can be a milestone in the awakening process. Information is easily attained, and clear and accurate once we are working through our own higher self.

I began to speak to my higher self by imagining me sitting across from myself. Of course I made her slimmer and younger looking! After a while, I just saw light, so I knew I was getting somewhere! Now, I can hear my higher self clearly. The soul connects us to God or our creator being, our I AM presence.

We come to Earth not as awakened souls but as volunteers to be tenants of this planet during this great Ascension time. You volunteered for this! You said sure, I want to be a part of the most amazing show in the galaxies! We Humans on Earth today are starseeds, teachers, healers and mothers/fathers birthing this New Earth. We enter sleeping but awake and remember at just the right time. We are seeded all over Earth, one or two to a family to anchor in the light. Many times, we are the black sheep of our biological family, a familiar story that most metaphysical people tell.

Nostradamus:
"Is Earth broken? Look around, what do you think? Human creator beings can manifest a new, free, thriving planet. Continue to pull back the curtain on motives and be extremely focused on patterns. Why would you want it any other way?"

Begin to build your own city on New Earth in your mind and thrust your destiny forward. You are the next rampart which fortifies and defends this new system of life. We can sense New Earth within the 5D timeline. Our bodies react to the frequency upgrade with ascension symptoms, or what some call "the ascension flu." As the light passes through your body, your frequency adjusts and it can respond with headaches, muscle aches, pressure, pain or other symptoms. Of course, if you are feeling these symptoms and want to rule out any health issue, consider consulting a doctor or holistic practitioner.

Saint Germain:
"You must know that when you speak up, there will be many who do not understand you or see your vision. They will not hear your words in their hearts or minds. Speak anyway. It doesn't affect your mission one way or another, their reaction is about them and not you. Decide at this moment and move ahead. Will you be held back by others or ascend to your rightful place? Do not let your light dim, each one is responsible for their actions and words. Many will try to knock you off your post, do not let them! It is why you are insulated with your soul family now."

CHAPTER 7:

What is your body saying?

Why do we become ill? Trauma, past lives, looping thoughts and our own emotions can add to, and prolong, accidents and illness. Many of these answers can be found in your aura.

Your Aura

Your aura is comprised of seven layers:

- Etheric
- Emotional
- Mental
- Astral
- Etheric Template
- Celestial
- Causal

These layers are called the subtle bodies.

The nearest layer to your physical body is the etheric body, a magnetic field that anchors the astral body to the physical. This layer is associated with the root chakra. Each layer beyond is associated with its own chakra.

Psychics, healers and medical intuitives can see symbols in the energetic field that can be manipulated for healing. The energetic field is made up of your aura, chakras and nadi (or smaller chakras.)

The symbols denote a starting point for healing; something to add or remove, or a direction to follow or even a specific issue to work on. Every healer has a group of symbols she regularly works with in most every healing. Sometimes symbols are specific to the client.

It takes focus, practice and patience to be able to understand the symbols that show up in a healing. This is where your own intuition, guidance from your Team of Light (through your higher self) and the pendulum come in.

Imagine that healing yourself or working with another person on their health is like playing a video game or assembling a puzzle.

If a client comes to you for healing, permission is assumed but it's a good practice to ask if the healing may commence. This opens the energy. I never send healing over distance without requesting permission first. Some healers believe if you petition the higher self of anyone and get the OK, healing can be sent. I do not agree with this idea.

I imagine each client's energy field is like a Monopoly board. If I am working as a part of a team of healers, one healer might see the Park Avenue and Boardwalk symbols, whereas I am following the symbols near the Jail! Due to ability and timing, a healer can only assist when the client is ready to heal. The open flow, timing and readiness must be there. Each healing session might remove or adjust a layer. Or there may be a miracle.

Some of the Tools and Symbols I see in the Energetic Body:

Sword, shield, key, knife, chalice, crown, geometric shapes, colors, ribbon, rope, chains, other people, a composite body, birthday cake, hand positions, Rubik's cube, stop sign, boat, etc.

All of your higher skills can be used to speak to your body. First the intention to hear what the body wants to say must be present. It might sound like:

- "My intention is to speak to my body today. Body or body part, please let me know how you are feeling and what I can do to help."

- "I love you,stomach! Do you have stuck emotions today that we might look at and relieve?" And so on.

You may be surprised at what you hear or receive! Bring in the information you want and need by simply tuning in, asking and listening closely.

Stomach speaks:
"You are not paying attention! I've always wanted to speak! Focus for now. I do not like my diet. I do not like the state I'm in. I am angry. You don't put me first. You have stuffed emotions for years. Don't hold back, it doesn't work. Release all agitators from your diet. Eat food that is good for you so that you can be supported in your healing."

The Chief:
"Our dear, we visit on this occasion regarding your health. Please, bring yourself close as we shall show you a map. There are unknowns, so keep working towards a clean diet. There are many treasures up ahead."

Chapter 8:

Who are you, really?

In a healing or reading it always helps to understand where your soul originally came from. I explain this to clients by saying each of us has a hometown but not all of us live there for our whole lives. Our souls originate from so many places: Earth, Inner Earth, and off planet. We come from many other realms.

On the day I realized I can simply ask the client's higher self where they are from, everything became so much easier! I didn't take many classes or do much research during my early years as a healer, I just listened to my own guidance in the beginning. So when I needed to know something, it was shown to me. There is so much to learn from each realm's sons and daughters. When the sitter is told of their soul's origin, it will make sense and feel like home to them.

Are you a Galactic being from the stars? A Starseed that volunteered to come to Earth for this great awakening? You might be a Blue Ray, an Indigo or Crystal or Hybrid child. These names pertain to the time and place when your soul came to Earth. I arrived in the 1960s in this incarnation, I am a Blue Ray. Indigos came later and so on. Often Galactic souls feel displaced, as we do not fit in. If you are primarily of Earth, you may be a "salt of the earth" person, a grounded Earth Steward who cares deeply about the planet.

Spotting a person from the God/Goddess realm is very easy. They have a confident and commanding way about them and are supreme manifestors.

Humans whose souls originated in the Angelic realm are often the most empathic and sensitive of all. Angels tend to overdo for others in the name of love.

Elemental realm folk often resemble their fey ancestors right down to their pointed or unusually shaped ears. Elemental people often have high energy, a great sense of play, quick movements and love the outdoors.

Understanding who you are, where your soul came from, a bit about your past lives, why you chose your birthday and family, are subjects that have occupied the minds of metaphysical seekers for years.

Why Did You Choose Your Birthday?

We choose our birthday for our own soul's growth. Each Sun sign has its positive and negative traits. Of course, that said, everyone is completely different but there are some consistencies that show up in every sign, Aquarius to Leo, etc.

It's fun to find out what sign matches best for true love with our sign. It's instructive to find out that as an Aquarius, stubbornness is one of my traits!

Eventually, you'll get to a place where nothing is more important to you than your own healing and growth. But in the beginning, it sure is fun to know all about who you are and who you once were.

Your Mind. As We Think, We Create.

Energy is my first language. I trust it. Fear, anger and big emotions can make us believe anything and our monkey minds can lead us on a merry chase. Energy never dies and cannot be destroyed. Each of us must take responsibility and decide what frequency we are flowing out into the world. When we reach that step, we learn how to hold our frequency when triggered. It is our energetic responsibility.

Holding Your Own Frequency

I considered myself fortunate when Spirit showed me what I call the Trigger Scale. This scale shows my client's emotional frequency in a way I simply can't miss! On their face, I see numbers between 1-10. The lower numbers, 1 through 3, show that I must hold these clients gently with my "angel's hands" because they have many uncleared and painful triggers from emotional and traumatic events in this life and past lives. Numbers 4 through 7, show me the client has done some work in therapy (or energy work of some type) to begin to clear away, integrate or at least become aware that they can be triggered by situations and actions. Numbers 8 through 10, signify clients are ready for the next level of healing; clearly and directly spoken.

What Happens When You Reach Level 10?

When we have reached level 10, we are not ruled by our emotions. We realize how privileged we are to be here right now; we are the observer and can use the observer stance to learn. We are an independent player in this game called humanity.

Becoming The Observer

How do we learn to observe and not react to every little thing? It seems hard, but once you learn to do it and practice, it's easy! Stay in your own beautiful, authentic heart and hold no attachments to any outcome. Flow from your heart space and blast that love out!

We pay for our own schooling one way or the other, don't we? Whenever we do more than we should for another person, feel sorry for someone, label something or someone, we stick to it. Freedom lies in observing what is in front of you and continuing to only work on that which is your job. Everyone else's "stuff" is not your job!

The Entrained Mind and Heart

When our minds and hearts come together and we process through both at the same time, we are able to access information with compassion, forgiveness and surrender. When this happens, we have less of a chance to ping pong off one another's emotions.

The Ho'oponopono

The ho'oponopono forgiveness and reconciliation prayer is valuable to use at any time in your healing journey. Ho'oponopono means "correction" and traditionally the words are spoken to clear the way between people and heal relationships. Remember, forgiveness is for US.

- I'm sorry.
- Please forgive me.
- Thank you.
- I love you.

Sometimes I add "I forgive myself."

Often, we do not think to forgive ourselves, but the energetic correction that happens when we do is beautiful to see; when we realize we can forgive ourselves for past behaviors. We must be ready to take a good hard look at our part in every relationship and situation and remember when we do, we become able to make a stand and realize we are sovereign beings with our own power. We are ready to receive the miracles that will surely happen. Living in gratitude and taking responsibility is a major part in healing.

Sometimes we need to heal the way between two people. Have you ever considered writing a love letter?

The Love Letter:

- This is what I love about you!
- Thank you for sharing your life and family with me.
- Thank you for all of the lessons, great and small that I learned when we were together.
- Thank you for helping me grow and being by my side.
- Thank you for loving me.

Don't forget to declare love for yourself.

I Declare:

Because I am a beloved child of God, I declare that I am a sovereign being, an independent power unto myself.

- I am free and therefore, as a free soul, I choose love for myself as my overriding frequency.

- I work diligently each day to integrate my story, as I know that my thoughts flow into the collective and so I hold energetic autonomy.

- I safely feel and release lower emotions as I integrate the reason why I had them in the first place.

- Because I am a beloved child of God and a sovereign being, I choose to send all lower frequencies that I am aligning with at this moment back to Source through grounding and intention, with love.

Chapter 9:

Overthinking and the Monkey Mind

We know that where we place our thoughts, energy grows. We have all had the experience of going to the grocery store when we are in a bad mood. Invariably, we perceive others are also in a bad mood when most of the shoppers are just simply thinking their own thoughts that have nothing to do with us. Our emotions color how we view people, places and even the products we purchase. There is a zillion dollar industry out there just making sure we have positive feelings about those products we buy.

Sometimes it's enough to recognize that we are in overthinking mode. Recognizing this is the first step. But when overthinking is entrenched, like having a song stuck in your head all day, there are other options for slowing down looping thoughts.

Can we stop overthinking at all? Hardly! But we can learn to relax our minds with music, learn to meditate and become an observer.

The Five-Point Brain Adjustment

Most clients require a five-point brain adjustment. Positions one through five clear the old business of the past, looping thoughts, emotions, difficulty sleeping, limited beliefs and depression/anxiety.

Why does this clearing work? Sometimes, just highlighting issues is enough for a client to begin to take responsibility and work on a situation that has been coming up for them. This 5-point adjustment brings up the issue and smooths the energy. The intention and clearing that comprises the five-point brain adjustment will be demonstrated in class.

The Sterling Way

Can we simply intend every day to have a good day? I believe we can. I call this thinking "sterling", as in holding a sterling heart or sterling thoughts. We endeavor to pull in the positive rather than sit in the less than positive. Can we decide to stop labeling our experiences? Yes, but what if you are around people whose frequency runs low or they see life in a negative way? Firstly, hold no judgment. Remember, we can't change another human and trying is exhausting! We also are not meant to get in the way of another's path.

What if your partner or friend is a narcissist or a victim/bully? Narcissists are very focused on themselves, put themselves first, love attention and often attract empaths. Much has been written about this narcissist/empath relationship. Putting yourself first will be your focus.

Being positive and focused on joy is not "spiritual bypassing" if there is work being done on one's shadow self or darker side of the unknown. Spiritual bypassing happens when a person is not willing or is unable to look at their shadow side. We all hold both dark and light within us.

When we get to a point where we choose our own self overall, there is usually a cost. But the payoff can be a brand-new life and better health.

The way we process information is linked with our emotions and is in combination with what we've learned in this lifetime (and what we brought forward from past lives). Add to it, what's going on in our physical body, along with what we learned from family and those around us early on, causes us to react to situations in a certain way.

Cognitive dissonance may be in play and nothing anyone says to us can allow the mind to change. It is entrenched. When there is cognitive dissonance, a person feels very uncomfortable when another way of looking at things is brought forward.

Merlin the Alchemist:
"You did your best; this individual does not wish to hear anything other than what she believes. You have adjusted the energy and the record went back to skip. It is not your place to assist any further."

Companion Guide:
"You cannot change others; it is not your job. They are stuck. This doesn't mean they always will be. Stay in peace. Today is a good day, is it not? Then stay in your own lane."

Do not harm yourself with thoughts of what you should have or could have done in the past. Each soul is on his or her own path. When we recognize that our frequency drops when we are in certain places, situations or around some individuals, it is up to US to make a change. Sit with why you are uncomfortable. Heal what is within yourself. Then go back and observe again.

Releasing Words:

- I release all hitchhikers, entities, artificial intelligence, implants, nanobots, "bugs", cords to another human or astral entity, old ET interference, scaffolding around me from past life bodies, wiring or blockages in time, space and matter.

- I release all contracts, agreements, vows, self-inflicted sabotage, energetic darts, weapons, curses or blockage placed within my field by another person or entity.

- I release toxins from my body and my hair, my brain, all organs, muscles, bones and cells. I neutralize all lower frequencies in ease, neutrality and love.

- I release all spells, booby traps, slingshots, memory erasures and any agreements I made freely or under duress from all timelines, past and present.

- I release all historic events that caused trauma to my body or energetic field including accidents or childbirth trauma, operations, vaccines, heavy metals and drugs.

- I call in divine doctors, nurses, chemists, and alchemists to assist me in releasing any foreign intervention in my body or energetic field.

- My frequency is tuned, and my body is filled with love.

The Truth. I See a 6, You See a 9

Saint Germain reminds us to stay in the heart when trying to understand if something is true or not. How does your body feel when asking the question? Did you ask your higher self?

Saint Germain also reminds us that sometimes perfectly accepted statements and ideas contain both the truth and the ego or motivation of the person or collective speaking. Use discernment to find your own truth. Empaths have a bit of trouble with what is true because usually they can see multiple sides. Is empathy a gift or a curse? Only you can say. Only you can say what is your own truth.

You Come First.

Can you speak up? If you receive the wrong change at the coffee stand, can you speak up and say so? What about when a friend speaks ill of you? Can you ask them why they did it? What about when it's time to release a friendship or say goodbye to a lover? Have you stayed too long at a job? Learning to speak up is imperative for good health.

A close look at what you believe about your work, relationship or family may be in order.

- Do you come first or does your job or family?

- What about your friends or everyone else?

Good for you if you answered yes, I come first! It's a matter of making the right decision in the best spirit. You don't need to raise your voice in anger. In fact, this may cost your body too much. Do your best and practice.

Another reason to keep your frequency high is for good immune health. There's nothing like fear or anger to compromise the immune system. There is no separation between what you think and your immune system. In fact, your overall health responds to how you think. Easy acceptance equals easy flow.

Your organs hold emotions. Negative emotions can attract toxins and viruses, especially fear. Think about how much fear you have felt and held onto in your life. Your kidneys and bladder hold onto fear, terror, conflict and the feeling of being unsupported. Every cell and organ has a consciousness. Your liver will hold on to anger, hatred, guilt and frustration and so on throughout your whole system.

Worrying can be a precursor to illness. The ego wishes to be in charge! People feel safer in control. Imagine observing a kinked hose. Some water will flow through the hose even if it's held tight. But all water, if we release the kink, can flow without constriction. Release, speak up, and flow.

Peace in the Forest Meditation

- Hold peace as your intention.
- Close your eyes, sit with your hands and feet apart for good energy flow.
- Pay attention to your breath, notice your abdomen rise on the in breath.
- Imagine you are walking on a path through a forest.
- Watch your bare feet as you walk along the ancient path.
- Up ahead is a huge clearing, stop at the opening.
- Notice the beautiful ring of cedar trees and the green grass.
- Step onto the grass and feel how cool and soft it is.
- Turn to the right and begin to walk around the perimeter of the path.
- As you pass from one cedar tree to the next, notice that there are forest animals peering out at you.
- See the birds in the trees, rabbits in the grass, deer laying under the sheltering branches. Pay attention to who comes for you.
- Intend to meet the angels, let them know you would like a peaceful healing.
- Ask the angels to touch you, speak to you or give you a sign.
- Allow the angels to take it from there.

Rest for 15 minutes with the angels in this peaceful place.

CHAPTER 10:
Hold your frequency

Imagine that you have had a good day. You sit down for a rest and realize that suddenly you're overcome with a feeling of sadness and grief. Ask yourself if this emotion is yours. Were you triggered earlier or were you reminiscing about a deceased loved one? Were you traveling through a town you used to live in during an earlier part of your life when you had trauma? Or are you picking up another person's emotions?

The Collective Consciousness

If you are an empath, you will be very aware of feeling the energy and emotions of your collective. This can be your soul family or group you are associated with, or it can be everyone on the Earth. People who are aligned with Earth's ever-changing energy may feel earthquakes or weather events before they happen.

Emotions

At the heart of every symptom or illness is an unhealed emotional pattern or loop. Bodies reflect what is happening in our minds. As within, so without. We punish our own bodies with the hot and cold emotions of anger, fear and resentment leading to resistance without even knowing that we are adding to our "story".

> ***Companion Guide:***
> *"Be as a little child, get sad and angry. That is the way out."*

In the late 1980s I took part in a personal and professional development program which at that time was called The Forum, now called Landmark. This work "uncovers the mechanisms that keeps us from being present to life" and it was the very first time I heard how our "story" impacts us. We all have stories about ourselves and the big players and events in our lives. These days we know that being present in the moment that is happening right now defines how our day goes and how life unfolds for us. Holding our thoughts in the present moment can cause all types of stress to melt. Do you find yourself constantly thinking of a death or personal loss of a job or relationship? This behavior sticks us firmly in the past.

Get Out of Your Own Way!

Companion Guide:
"Your mind needs to peel off and run wild. Let it go! We wish you the joy of unbridled thought and creativity. Your guidance team sees your earthly struggle and pain and the ease to step out of it. You have not quite figured it out yet and it is so simple! You shall laugh when you realize it. You can transmute this pain with play. Your small self didn't play much."

When you take great care of yourself, believe in yourself and put yourself first, slowly those around you may come to see you in a different light. We must set our own boundaries and practice them. Occasionally, people will entrain up with you as your frequency rises. They might change. Or they won't. The focus must be on one's self.

Are you the one everyone calls when they need something? Maybe they need to rant or need help moving or deciding on something. Draw the line! I tell my clients next time this happens, stand your ground. If you are having a rest day or self-care day or are busy with absolutely anything, do not put anyone else before you! No matter who it is, tell them you must stay at home and wash your cat. Even if you do not have a cat. This might take practice!

Comparing yourself to someone else and putting yourself at the end of the line can cause you to not only get stuck but to miss opportunities. When we're willing to see our behavior as a response to trauma, we understand that for us to heal, we must take a close look at what has happened to us. Taking that close look, doing your own work and clearing it, is the difference between creating a story about it and holding onto the trauma, versus healing.

When you are ready, making time for yourself and choosing yourself as your first priority might look something like this:

- I practice my spiritual skills every day.
- I ground and clear myself each day.
- I eat well and drink enough pure water every day.
- I make sure I am not too tired, too hungry or too overwhelmed and if I am, I eat, drink, rest, ground and I speak up!
- I reach out to friends regularly.
- I write down my thoughts in a journal daily.
- I go outside in nature.

The Violet Flame of St. Germain:

- I imagine that I am standing in the Violet Flame. I feel at peace as it flows around me.
- I feel the Violet flame flow through my body and into the room I am sitting in.
- I see the Violet flame traveling through my home, and out into my yard. I see it move along my street.
- I flow the Violet Flame into my town and county.
- I visualize the Violet Flame over my state and into the United States or the country I live in.
- I bring myself back into my body and notice the Violet Flame around my body.
- Within the Violet flame, I integrate any mask I have worn to fit in.
- I release any face I wear to please someone other than myself.
- I release anytime I dumbed myself down in any situation.
- I rise within the Violet Flame and claim my own sovereignty.

The Pain Body

As we grow up during our first seven years, we are closely observing the people around us. We take on another person's beliefs as truth, and behaviors as our own without being conscious of it. Children's eyes and brains are wide open and do not know a different way to be.

What happens if there were no examples of people to trust or if you did not learn how to play or have fun while you were growing up? Many of us grew up in families that shamed us. Did you arrive in your new life full of fear that you just cannot put your finger on? Remember, you called in your large themes, your family and birthday and sometimes even brought forth past life issues to re-sort in this lifetime. This can include fears and other emotions that make no sense to you and may be coming from a past life memory.

Take a rigorous inventory of your own beliefs. Do you still believe the things you learned in your early life are *your* truth? Or was it someone else's closely held belief that raised you? Has limited thinking stopped you at any time? We perceive others as *we* think and observe. That is exactly how they perceive us!

The pain body, according to Eckert Tolle, is an energetic form attached to us through ego. To me, it looks like a red copy of the client's own body, just slightly overlaid to the physical form. It is created by an emotional loop of anger, fear, resentment and shame etc. that is held in place by emotions and thoughts. It's an actual entity that feeds on these emotions that run over and over, like a tape recording. It just doesn't work to try to outthink the pain body. A simple awareness of it and ongoing observation is the beginning of release.

For example, an individual with a drug or alcohol problem may have a story that they are all alone. Anger comes up, over and over, and the individual manipulates people to stay away. This justifies their belief that they are alone, which justifies drinking or using.

Recognize how you feel when you begin to tell your story. If you find yourself constantly referring to the old days when you were sick, what you have survived or where your body hurts and all the ways in which you are exhausted or anxious, that is what builds the pain body and it works at keeping us from being present when we are identified with the illness or the story. How does the pain body get triggered? And how do we stop identifying with our story of illness and trauma?

The culture of illness in the United States is easy to see. Every other TV commercial is touting a new drug or vaccine. The television blasts out that the "flu season" is beginning in September each year and that is kept up until spring when "allergy season" comes around again. We are beginning to see where stories have been accepted as fact. When we spend all of our focus on what is wrong, we draw in the frequency of illness.

Arcturian Healing

- Hold healing as your intention.
- Close your eyes and sit with hands and feet apart for energy flow.
- Call in the Arcturians.
- Pay attention to your breath, notice your abdomen rise on the in breath.
- Imagine an ocean that stretches as far as you can see in both directions.
- Notice the weather and the sky.
- Observe that the path you are on has turned from sand into sky blue topaz, smooth and sparkling under your bare feet.
- As you walk on the topaz path, turn left and walk parallel to the water.
- Stop and call in the Sun from overhead and see yourself in the column of golden light.
- Intend to walk into your merkaba or ship of light.
- When you enter, notice the color around you.
- Ask for a message from the Arcturians.
- Spend time resting in the energy.

What is Collective Consciousness?

If you are an empath, you will be very aware of feeling the energy of your collective. This can be your soul family or a group you are associated with. It can be everyone on the Earth.

Every healer and reader has been asked the question, "Who is my soulmate?" The term soulmate is often misunderstood as only being one's romantic partner. I've met a handful of soulmates who live together harmoniously, and I've met many who return together in this lifetime to work out their issues as mirrors to one another. The best reason I've ever heard from spirit as to why past life souls are reunited is for love. That is a reason to make us happy!

Have you ever met a person and known deep within your heart that you have been together before? They feel like home. They may be a part of your soul family. A person, who seems to be very special to you, can also be a piece of your very own soul. Even a twin flame doesn't have to be a romantic partner. Your twin flame is your number one mirror in this lifetime, one half of your soul split into two. Sometimes it works out that you fall in love with your twin and marry this individual. Sometimes this relationship is in play so that you can learn the lesson as mirrors, and you move on to another relationship.

Mugged in the Astral Plane

When we wake up after a night's sleep and feel like we've been hit by a bus, we may feel as if we've been working all night long instead of slumbering. What happened? All humans travel in the astral realm when sleeping. Just what we're doing out there is up to debate, but we can make some broad guesses. If you are from the Angel realm you are usually helping in some way during sleep; maybe you are directing, healing or counseling. You could be fighting! Think about laying down your weapons. This can cause peace to flow into your daytime interactions.

Astral travel has been much debated. Is your daytime life, real life or is dream time reality? I believe that astral travel filters debris from the human energy field by going over old situations, relationships and trauma and causes the entire energetic system to clear; a review prior to clearing or integration, in other words. Remember, past, present and future are occurring simultaneously.

The astral plane feels different these days than it used to. With the Ascension there is a lot going on! Do astral attacks still happen? Of course they do. Prayer and statements prior to going to sleep are encouraged as well as raising our frequency to clear fear patterns and old beliefs. Why would someone/thing attack you on the astral plane?

A person or astral entity, who is an old enemy in this life or a past life, may consciously or unconsciously try to attach to your energy field and cause you to become weak or ill. Identify bad blood between you and others in your current life. Remember to use the Ho'oponopono to clear the way. Always remember, forgiveness is for YOU.

Since we spend about one third of our life sleeping, it's best to have a great sleep hygiene routine along with practices we honor prior to going to bed.

Sleep Hygiene

- Turn off electronic devices an hour before bed and do not store them in your bedroom.
- Limit exercise an hour before bed.
- Go to bed about the same time every day.
- Keep your bedroom clean and clear of clutter.
- Add crystals such as rose quartz, obsidian and labradorite for sleep.

Chapter 11:

Past Lives

Meeting someone that you have known from a past life is an amazing feeling. It feels like you've known this person forever! It's all about the growth of your own soul or theirs, if you are back together again. Relationships can continue from one lifetime to another. There are many reasons souls decide to incarnate together. It is all for the soul's growth as we know, but happily, souls return for the pure love experience, too. If two souls decide to meet again, it also can be that one is learning the lesson and the other is holding space.

A past life reading is worth considering when one has health issues or ongoing emotional strife. Many times the origin of what is bothering you can be pinpointed and integrated. Occasionally, just knowing that something has happened in a past life that can be traced to an issue that is happening right now, is enough to bring about healing.

If I find a past life issue during a session that is ready to be viewed, cleared and integrated, I will begin to look at emotions. The client's higher self will show me an unreleased emotion or symbol. For example, sometimes it is fear, anger or self-loathing, that comes up for the client and they are not even aware of why they are feeling that way. It is just sudden. Of course it needs to be ruled out that the emotion does not belong to someone else and is being empathically picked up by the sitter. The question can be asked "Do you have fear or anger or another emotion that you do not understand or that comes on suddenly, out of nowhere?" It may be time to look at past lives.

The Akashic Records and the Halls of Amenti

Inspired by my conversation with Tracy Williams, medium, dream teacher, soul mentor and energetic practitioner.

A psychic medium can see important past lives, but everyone can travel (through meditation or hypnosis) to the Akashic Records, the global library of all soul's incarnations. It is a recording of all you have accomplished in every life, all your thoughts and ideas. The Halls of Amenti hold information about all universal, galactic realms.

The Akashic Records and the Halls of Amenti are interdimensional places. One can imagine your soul's information is uploaded to the cloud just like photos from your gallery on your smartphone!

We travel to the Records with our spirit guides, as well as guides who will assist us once we are inside. When I travel to the Akashic Records, I see a building that looks a lot like the Tacoma Post Office! The trail to the post office shows me much about a person's own path. As we travel along the path we might make energetic adjustments. All kinds of information is shown to me, to reveal to the sitter as we walk toward the halls. Once inside the building, we walk down the long hallway until we get to the exact door that houses the sitter's records. The sitter opens the door and what is inside the room reveals as much about them as their blueprint does.

It is valuable to read your path (happening now), timeline (this lifetime) and blueprint (soul's origin). Most sitters wish to read their blueprint for contracts and information regarding their purpose. I am a bottom-line kind of person! So I like to read the bottom line and find out who exactly the person is that I am helping. Contracts can be cleared or better understood if karma still requires the contract to be finished. Oftentimes the sitter wishes to do that. Karma comes into play when we are not aligned with our divinity.

Remembering who you are and what you have accomplished can be a lifelong journey. Your own path in this life can be viewed by traveling to these vibrational libraries. As you work on healing yourself and clearing away the debris, such as stuck emotions and old patterns, your frequency will rise. Your skills will accelerate as even more is revealed to you.

Holding Space

It's a pure act of love when one person observes and holds a loving space for another to heal or go through a hard energetic lesson. It happens in life and it can also be a decision made on the other side to be a divine witness for another person, family or group. Sometimes your perceived enemy here on Earth was a close friend or beloved soul from another lifetime who gave their intention to reincarnate with you this go around. If this is a new idea for you, you might wonder "Now what!?

This is why we are meant to be the observer. We cannot really hate anyone because they may be here to wake us into remembering who we truly are. Standing up for one's self is a theme often seen in a reading. You cannot compare yourself to another person because you are the only YOU! Comparing yourself can cause missed opportunities.

Mirror Affirmation for Every Day:

Hold the frequency of joy and smile to release endorphins.

Look directly at your face and whole body in the mirror and say:

- I am getting better looking every day!
- By golly, I am intelligent! I am strong!
- I believe you, I believe in you!
- You are my best friend.

- You are safe.
- My mission today is to put myself first.
- My purpose here on Earth is to bring in the light, I will do it easily and effortlessly and with great joy!
- I will do my best every day.
- I am loved.
- I AM worthy!
- I release all programs of lack and scarcity.
- I claim the abundance that is always available to me.
- I now allow in all the abundance that may have been blocked from me, in any way, from the recent past or during past lives.
- I bring in all manner of abundance easily and effortlessly.
- I'll pay what I owe.
- Money is energy and it flows easily towards me.
- I am worthy of good friends and supportive family.
- I am worthy of a good job that pays well and challenges me.

Growing Up

We started out as a very young sponge (child) soaking up what we see around us and completely believing that is the only way things are done! We spend the rest of our lives after those early days making our own way and releasing early programming and beliefs; sometimes even releasing family traditions or at the very least making them our own. In order to write ourselves a story we can live with going forward; the old stories must be purged or at least recognized and recalibrated.

I remember piping up in grade school that each of us humans required not only food, water and shelter but we needed love! Yes, I was that little weirdo.

Growing up, there were no words such as narcissist or gaslighting. I didn't know why I was different. Never heard the word empath. Just a little astrology, even just a bit, would've helped to understand what was happening around me. It took me years to recognize toxicity in early, ongoing relationships and name it for what it truly was. If you find yourself hanging in there for years and years thinking you might be able to "help" or change people… you cannot. The lesson of observation is a true art.

There are times lessons must be worked through with miles between you and the ones that harmed you, for safety and peace of mind. When you have reached a point where your healing, health and peace of mind comes first then maybe you can be around these people again. But when it is time to walk away, you will know that it is the right thing to do.

Words From a New Life

It is always a perfect time to give gratitude and more gratitude. The ho'oponopono goes a long way to clear space between souls. Of course, there are light codes for just that situation! But another way to clear the path with your ancestors and restore health is to unlock what holds you in an ancestral loop.

To those who harmed me, poked and nudged me to be someone I wasn't, I say thank you! To my teachers who taught me every day with compassion, I say thank you. To those who allowed me to learn at my own pace, to discover my own waking up, I say thank you. For the days I feel like I know something and the next day I realize I know nothing, I am so grateful. To those that hurt me over and over again until I chose myself, I say thank you. You were my greatest teacher.

Who knows what this new life will bring? I am feeling so grateful to realize I am whole, knowing that I understand just a little and that I am awake to all possibilities. I do not know everything, and I love the discovery. I feel the embodiment of my very core that I AM!

I chose me. I chose peace.

Sunny, our friend from the other side:
"Take your hangman's noose and remove it. Wear it as your Goddess crown. You are free. You have created a beautiful new life."

When it's Time to Walk Away

Trust yourself! You will know in your heart when it is time to walk away from friends, family, work experiences or anything that is not a 50-50 equal division and no longer supports your growth. Spirit shows us over and over, and in increasingly larger doses, when we are out of alignment with our own soul's path. These nudges are called red flags! And they get bigger and louder the more you do not pay attention to them.

Remember, holding onto something past it's "pull date" can cause looping. When we continue to stay in a situation with someone else such as a marriage or relationship "for the kids" or "just until the children graduate", there's a chance your red flag will grow larger and flappier.

Do you remember how you felt when a huge lesson was learned, and you moved on? Sweet relief. This can be yours again. It is never too late to choose yourself. Look straight on at the issue. Dig the problems out vigorously with love for yourself. No camping out in the past or even in the future. Firmly stay in the present.

Saint Germain:
"Your time to stand up on your own may be met with resistance. All must talk together about their feelings or one person's feelings will be left by the wayside. That is the usual way to stuff feelings into the body where they remain. You have a good chance right now, take a long look at all that you feel. Don't give up. You are giving up too easily. No one will know how you feel unless you tell them."

Psychic Attack

Goldfinger to James Bond:
"Once is happenstance, twice is coincidence. The third time is enemy action."

Goddess Kali:
"When emotions suffer, when you get tired or overwhelmed, you are exposed as low hanging fruit to people who are either jealous, evil or bored. This goes for everyone. People's machinations will come to light. No one likes the squeaky wheel; they will show up for who they are to the wrong person soon."

Jealousy is an emotion that doesn't really make much sense to me! But people sure do get jealous of one another. Oftentimes jealousy is a great motivator for psychic attacks when a fire is fanned into a flame. Maybe in another lifetime you took their man or woman. Maybe in this lifetime you just bug one another, or you have something they want.

Does it count as an attack if a person or group gets mad at you and spends days and months thinking about how mad they are? Yes. Because this can go on and on and emotions are easily sensed between people. Daggers of emotion coming at you, thrown with repressed anger or jealousy can hit you in your most receptive place, an old injury to a "soft spot" such as the back of your neck or stomach, etc. They can set up a smear campaign against you at your work or within your family or friendship circle. The target of this anger and hate can certainly feel the emotion coming at them.

What to do When You Realize You've Been Attacked

A psychic attack can come out of nowhere. It can begin when you are at home or in a public place, anywhere. An attack can be sent by an individual or mounted by a group. Suddenly, you feel pain in your neck, back or gut. You feel ill and exhausted. Perhaps these symptoms are ones you have had for months or years and simply cannot clear them, no matter what therapy or modality you use.

Another method of psychic attack can be created by a third-party. Skilled dark magicians or even people with a little bit of personal power and focused attention can send nefarious energy your way. Occasionally, an aspect of a person may send an attack that they are unaware of. The individual who has the aspect as a part of them may be unaware they are doing this. More often than not, if you are psychically attacked you will know who has sent the low energy and can clean it out of your field. In some cases, you may need the help of a healer.

How to Clear Psychic Attacks

Remember, low and negative energy sent by someone will land in your weak spot. If you've had an old injury or packed in old rotten emotions, there's the target! Once you recognize this has happened, you are armed for the future! If you feel it again, stop instantly and clear. Set your boundaries, armor.

You may have an old contract with the person who has slimed you. Remember, we all have dark and light within us. The energy being lobbed at you may be from someone who is just angry but still lets the daggers fly. Armor yourself, clear your energy. There are situations where it is appropriate to speak directly to someone about this. Get it out in the open, but only if you believe you are firm, clear and safe. Other times sending the energy back is the only option.

Subconsciously, do you feel sorry for them? That type of energy can keep their energy attached to you. Hold no fear or apprehension. You have the ability to recognize when an attack happens and also the ability to clear it yourself. The frequency of fear will rise and fall but we can hold a wall of peace. Trust your expanded light body.

Psychic attacks are a reality. We'll use the peanut butter and jelly sandwich for an example. If I hold a PB&J in my hand, I may get the peanut butter on me. If I shake your hand, it gets on you. We are light, just permeable sponges. We pick up other people's energy. It's just too easy to take our frustration and anger out on social media or on someone who has the bad timing to be in front of you when you blow up and the PB and J goes flying. This is an example of passing energy on. We can have an old trauma, get triggered and blow up.

What to do when you have been attacked:

- Identify where it has come from

- Is this past life or this life?

- Clear yourself and your space

- Armor yourself, your home and those who live in it, your car, your property, your business

- Choose well those who you allow into your energy

- Send the energy back by reflecting love

- Know that the light comes for everyone, but we still protect ourselves everyday

Chapter 12:
Awakening

Holy Mother Mary on Winter Solstice 2020:
"All are star and stone. Master and student. No awakened soul is set higher than any unawakened sleeper. All are bursting at the heart. So full of pain, grief, anger and yet, as the star of Bethlehem is near and with it the great galactic alignment with our portal Sun; all have the power and chance to release old emotions that have driven you and fly free! Ground into Mother, hear what she is saying. It sounds like I love you."

Archangel Metatron, 12/2017:
"These are glorious times that we are in, are they not? It might seem to you that Earth is spinning faster than before, because it is!

Gaia is shaking off what is no longer viable to her growth and expansion. An expanded reality is being created before your very eyes by you! Get used to it. This is a reality that will become clear to humanity as you all put it into practice.

Lightworkers, all of you are mirrors to those who are still sleeping. In simple terms, there is a ballast of humanity that will be released in order to bring about the new souls to support the next work. There is energy in pure form that will be released to continue the process. The recent hurricanes, earthquakes, fires, flooding and sickness are examples. Do not hold on to the vibration of pain and loss over these shifts. Allow the Earth's energy to move through you. Feel it in your body, acknowledge it and allow it to move on its way. You, as humans in this era, are bound up with the notion that you can control things. You cannot."

We must keep love in mind and be very patient with those souls who have recently awakened to remembering who they are. Sometimes, folks are on the fast track at the moment they wake up! But us OG spiritual/ metaphysical people who woke up early had to slog through heavy family disbelief and social programming with little support. We did it mostly on our own, until our spiritual family or soul family showed up. When those beautiful souls who hold our own frequency finally come to us, it's like every holiday, birthday and vacation rolled into one! It is like being suddenly home. Most of us hadn't felt "home" prior to that reunion.

Back in the day, there were fewer metaphysical bookstores and no internet! How did we meet like-minded people? I remember going to the library and checking out every book I could find on metaphysical subjects. Then I started to meet my own soul groups. What a relief. Suddenly it was possible to have conversations out loud that I could only dream of having since childhood. Suddenly, I had a pack to run with and people I could trust. Questions were not off-limits, and I felt like I had something to say. I felt free for the first time in my life.

Rev. Dr. Martin Luther King, Jr. on Timelines:
"The two busy sides dim and all that is before you is the middle road. This is seen with discernment and observation. The reason "now" feels off, is that what seems so real is disappearing and you personally have tried to look backwards. When you take your observation backwards to 3-D, you will get blinded again. Rightly so, it must occur a few, maybe many times for you to see how it works. Stay at a higher frequency. Observe the peace of the Free Road."

Keep looking for your soul family. They are out there, and you will know them because they feel like home. Metaphysical subjects can now be researched at any moment of the day. In the old days there were mystery schools. Now we have UFO groups and Sasquatch groups and Reiki shares, paranormal conventions, healing centers and meet ups. The sky is the limit! It's easier than ever to find both information and like-minded people.

Check out your town's Spiritualist church or call a bookstore. Most bookstores are great resources for what's going on in your community. If you live in a small town without much happening metaphysically, it may be time for you to create your own meetup, psychic panel or metaphysical fair.

Channeling

The regenerative codes and the messages from Spirit in this book have been channeled by me over the past four years.

Channeling is simply opening oneself up with intention to connect to spirit and aligning your frequency to the frequency of that spirit. We as humans align with the frequency of the thought and the transmission that comes through. It can contain a simple proclamation of love, information for other people, teaching about metaphysical subjects or my favorite, good old-fashioned support.

I love it when my Team of Light, seemingly out of the blue, connects with me for nothing but love and support that sounds something like this:

"We love you! You did well today. We are holding you in the highest light of peace and love."

Or my favorite, *"You are tired. Go take a nap."*

It is so uplifting and can be just the balm your spirit needs. Better yet, they may tell you some teeny, little tidbit they witnessed you doing today. I love it when they say "I like your new hairstyle" or "The new color of paint looks great in the kitchen." We are never alone and they prove it.

Mediumship

There are five categories of mediumship or channeling of spirit: mental, trance, transfiguration, physical and physical healing. Mental mediumship or connecting with Spirit through the mind is most common. Conscious, mental channeling occurs when the medium is aware of information coming through. The medium's conscious mind must "step to the left" as my Guide taught me. There are many ways to learn how to do this.

Trance mediumship is done by achieving a very relaxed state and intending to go "somewhere else." Often, the medium remembers very little, if anything, afterwards. The mind of the medium is focused on something completely different and the spirit speaks through the mouth of the medium.

Transfiguration channeling is done by achieving a very relaxed state. With permission, the deceased or spirit guide will enter the channel's body; transfiguring the face or body with their energy or ectoplasm, (the substance that is produced in the body of the medium and flows during channeling). This type of transfiguration channeling can be seen by people observing the seance especially in a red lighted room. A darkened room using only red light allows people to see the being come through easily.

Physical mediumship occurs when the medium is able to produce a substance such as ectoplasm or an aportation through their own body such as crystals or coins. This type of mediumship is rare and an amazing process to witness

During physical healing mediumship, spirit guides from all realms will step forward. They will point out what needs to be healed in the person I am working with. I channel the energy of healing at the same time the spirit guide is either holding the frequency or sending a higher one.

During channeling, I tend to see my Companion Guide, who is very special to me, take me dancing. Clearly this is something we did in a past life, because in this life I am a major klutz. But it feels wonderful to dance with him while my mind is elsewhere. My guide has shown me our life together in great detail. It is like a waking dream.

I see beings from all realms, as well as, the deceased. They stand before me in my heart field and I hear them speaking in my mind. It is clear to me that the information is coming from them. It takes practice for mediums to learn to bring through solid, meaningful evidence. It was very important to me that I hear and translate the words correctly, so I worked for years with a variety of spirit guides to be able to hold my frequency and focus while channeling. This is the deceased person's chance to clear their unfinished business, give a special greeting to a loved one or prove that life goes on. This is our chance, as a medium, to be a small part of a truly loving gift to a grieving friend or family member.

It is most important not to censor the information coming through. Mediums cannot possibly understand everything a spirit is saying. So we just describe what we see, hear and feel. I now only channel through my higher self and I employ a gatekeeper so that my energy is not compromised. My father on the other side is my gatekeeper and he does a beautiful job at keeping everyone who wishes to speak from the other side in order. This allows me to focus on one message at a time.

Call in the Holy Ones Prior to Channeling:

- In divine peace, I call in Creator God, my Team of Light, my beloved ancestors and my own guides and guardians through my higher self, in the highest light.

- Please allow for open hearts and minds as I humbly ask to be a clear channel of messages in love and peace.

Automatic Writing

Early on I taught myself to write with Spirit. I still use this technique when I need to give a copy of the message to a sitter or when I'm told to write a message down. It's very easy to do with practice. The information comes in easily in flow, without conscious thought. I believe the writing practice helps the medium's spoken channeling because one focuses with precision on the words needing to come out. Just like the old game of "telephone," a message can get corrupted or broken down. It is always very important to say exactly what Spirit or the deceased wants to say!

Again, moving your thoughts to the left is the way I learned to channel. Of course, thoughts can be moved to the right. There are many techniques to simply get your mind out of the way. Once you understand how to do that, it happens automatically. Relax, trust and practice.

When Spirit speaks it does not sound like the medium's words. The communication is of highest quality, positive, often simple and always beautifully said. If you are hearing negative messages, instantly and lovingly command to clear yourself. Ground. Raise your vibration and try again another time.

Sometimes, corrupted messages come in. If you can imagine a scenario where you and a friend are deep in conversation and another person inserts themselves into your visit. This is similar to what happens on the spiritual plane. There is no reason to fear communication with spirit guides or the deceased. After all, there is no time, all is occurring at the same time, past present and future. Sometimes the being you are communicating with, is just you from another dimension! We may have an agreement from a past life to work with a particular being. Do not censor yourself. Release the words they give you and let go of it. Speedy writing seems to help. If you go slowly, you have more time to censor yourself.

Remember, *we* are multidimensional, and the spirit guide you are speaking with is of equal value to you. This is how the spirit realm wishes to be seen, including hierarchy. Our job and theirs cannot be done, to the highest degree and best outcome, without one another.

How to Begin to Channel

Declare that you are ready to learn to channel. Decide which type of channeling you will focus on. Clear yourself thoroughly as well as the room where you will be channeling. Call in your divine team, stating that you only call in those of the highest light.

- I declare that I am ready to learn to channel.

- I call in Source, my Team of Light: my angels, guides, and beloved ancestors.

- Say the name of who you wish to communicate with or be open to your guidance team.

- Light a candle, if you wish, to draw the spirit forward that you are petitioning.
- Use every higher skill you already have available.
- Keep your mind open, do not censor yourself.
- Take notes afterwards so you can track your progress.

Nostradamus
"Channeling each day prevents worrying! Why do you worry? Precisely, you've learned to! Time to unlearn it. You feel so odd because you are between worlds! We are watching and admiring how much all of you put up with every day!"

How Does it Feel to Channel?

Depending on who you are and your skill set, you may hear, see, feel or sense the spirit guide or beloved deceased. To me, channeling feels like meditation. My body relaxes and I prepare to view "the movie." Make sure you choose a peaceful place to call in Spirit. Set up a crystal grid to support and clear the space with light, sage or Palo Santo.

You may wish to ask for a symbol that your guide is with you when you are ready to receive channeling. The symbol can be anything and it will come through you in any one of your skills. When I channel, I see color or sense the presence of those who wish to speak. The frequency may feel like pressure on your chest or head or you may notice hair standing up on your arms.

I see diamond light for Kwan Yin, blue for Archangel Michael and other galactic beings depending on the hue; rainbow colors for the unicorns, golden light for Archangel Metatron and Ascended Master Kuthumi. When I am having a visit from my own beloved deceased family or friends, I have seen yellow flowers, yellow butterflies or white butterflies.

Remember the deceased are non-embodied people who are just like us. Just because they are dead does not mean they are all seeing and knowing. Pick well who you choose to listen closely to and use your own discernment when channeling. Spirit and the deceased come through with their own agenda. Sometimes it's just love. I make the statement that I am willing to speak to the highest self of any deceased person who will come through. If you are bringing through a person who has just passed away, you may be speaking to the soul prior to learning and changing. After time has passed, you are likely to speak to a more evolved soul. Set aside your ego. As you channel, body sensations and mind chatter simply fall away.

The Gatekeeper

You may wish to ask for a gatekeeper who can usher in souls or spirit one at a time. This is done to keep your energy flowing and stable and to help manage souls from overamping your energy field. Deceased family and friends are often so excited that you are getting ready to hear their words! They bend over backwards to get their message to us. When it's time, they are ready. The gatekeeper is very helpful if you expect several members of your deceased family to come through, and imperative if you are channeling those you do not know for someone else.

I do not allow a deceased person to channel through my body. I make this known prior to channeling and make a strong statement. Sometimes it happens that a very insistent spirit will try and I lovingly command them out of my body. I also make the same statement to my guides early on. As you can imagine, energy can be left behind during channeling. It is most important that you are grounded prior to starting, ground after the channeling and completely clear yourself before you close down the energy. Then, always remember to thank the Spirits that came in to assist you. I am very grateful to my spirit guides and my father. It is so much easier on the physical body to have souls come through one at a time.

It is most important to drink water prior to channeling and support your body afterwards with rest, hydration and food. We must honor and respect the channeling and our own body.

Nostradamus:
"The need to employ a gatekeeper is important for your energetic flow. The description you gave of the feeling of a "free-for-all" during mediumship is acknowledged, hence the stepping up of your father. This happened sooner rather than later and we are ready to give you some direction."

Ghosts on Board

The deceased are attracted to the light of the living. You may be a person that attracts souls. If you suddenly feel heavy, depressed or tired you may have a ghost or discarnate (nonphysical) being within your energy field or home. As mediums, our "heart light" shines brightly. Deceased souls who wish to get a message to a loved one often seek us out.

Ghosts may not be aware that they have died. Their death may have been sudden, such as an accident, or even a killing, and they can wander or stick in a place that is important to them such as their former home or business. They may replay a certain event or reflect a certain place in time. Sometimes they are attracted, just like entities, to your beautiful energy.

Earthbound Spirits, Entities and Attachments

Entities will suck your energy like food. They are also attracted to dead or lower frequency spots in your energetic field caused by emotions such as anger and fear.

Every healer will eventually encounter attachments and entities when working with clients. These spiritual attachments are an everyday part of healing and can be cleared easily, calmly and with neutrality and love.

Energy hygiene or energy autonomy must be taught to the client as a daily part of clearing. It is not enough to simply ground and clear your chakras every day! The energy on Earth has moved us into needing a whole new level of energy clearing. When people begin to awaken and sense that they are multidimensional beings and begin to travel a metaphysical path, there are choices to be made as far as taking care of themselves every day.

Trauma, thought forms, family issues and addictions can create a "landing space" for entity attachment. We resist going into our dark spaces and yet the energy and our own growth demands it!

Regular energetic clearing and metaphysical practices along with a strong belief system that includes the knowledge that anyone can release an entity back to the light with love; keeps us in the moment and completely unworried about entity attachment. After all, we release them back to God in love.

I am a "psychopomp" or soul guide. Souls are drawn to me and I assist them to cross over. Whenever I am led either by a client, or by the understanding that a soul is around me (by acknowledging the signs,) I offer a crossing to the soul, and all souls, that are within one mile of me and within one mile of the client if we are meeting remotely. Sometimes it is a huge group. I consider it one of the most beautiful and touching ceremonies to take part in.

Every healer has a special skill. It will become apparent what your best skill is if you spend time working on yourself and those people around you that are open and asking for your assistance. Learn from others and make your special skill your own. The more you practice, the easier and more powerful the work will become.

Reincarnation and Your Life Path

If you can read your path, timeline or blueprint, or have it read to you during a past life reading or QHHT hypnosis session, you can find out what your lessons are this time around, as well as who the big players are that join you in life's journey. Your path, as I see it, shows the challenges you are working with now. When we call for information regarding our timeline, we will see information from this lifetime. When we view our blueprint, we may see anyone of our lives back to the origin of our souls. This can be done through viewing the Akashic records or Halls of Amenti records with a skilled healer/medium. I see this type of information in a reading when it comes up for a sitter and they are ready to release contracts and cords with individuals and groups. Specific symbols come up that shows the sitter is ready for timeline information to be brought forth.

Reincarnation
Professor Einstein:
"There have been countless lifetimes that have passed to create this one life, the one you are having in the body at this present moment. Cherish this life! For many countless breaths have passed through the you that you are. Imagine how many people you have loved, touched, and how many souls love you. When I heard people say in my day that the soul lives but once, I shook my head. I could not grasp the shortsightedness and I believed with every particle of myself that the soul continued. Then of course, I proved it in my lifetime. The light is all, everything that we need to concern ourselves with. In it lives all life."

Welcoming a new baby into your family is a wonderful occasion. But what if the son or daughter was once your mother in another lifetime? Reincarnation is accepted by most cultures these days. Books such as many Lives, Many Masters by Brian Weiss and books by Dolores Cannon have helped people to understand the concept of reincarnation, past lives and what happens to the soul between lives.

Babies choose their family and sometimes it's because of a needed lesson for soul growth for either baby, parent or sibling. Channeling can be done with the baby in utero and fascinating information can come up. General information regarding the health of the baby, disposition or general traits, as well as information about other family members can be disclosed. It is a beautiful experience to hear the "voice" of the child prior to delivery, if there have been concerns about the health of mother or baby.

Suicide

I lost my dear friend to suicide in 2018. It was a shock, and I was devastated. Several days after the news of her death, I received a beautiful card written by my friend. She thanked me for our years of friendship together. We had fun on trips and just hanging out. We spent holidays together and we helped people together. She was a giver and a person who thought of others. She was my teacher for so many things!

About a week after her death, she appeared to me in spirit. I was sitting in my kitchen writing my small part of her eulogy. She said she could now feel the love being sent to her but when she was on Earth she "just didn't get it!" Through her trademark gentleness and humor she helped me to understand that she felt hopeless here on Earth. She couldn't see a way out. In retrospect, her death released her soul at the correct time for her blueprint. I see her as a golden angel now that still helps me and so many others.

It is devastating to lose a loved one to suicide. It is not a time to blame them or anyone else or worry about their soul. Every person I've ever spoken to on the other side who has killed themselves has crossed over. Sometimes they need help crossing, but they are united with family and their own Spirit Team.

My Companion Guide
"Do not harm yourself with thoughts of what you could've done, she was gone from you and could not be reached."

Orbs

Spirit orbs are a paranormal phenomenon of both human, spirit and animal origin that show up in photos or videos and can sometimes be seen by the naked eye and are commonly found both indoors and out. Orbs can appear any color; translucent, white, silver, blue and rainbow. In homes and businesses with paranormal activity, there can be a lively presence of orbs that can be shown on video. Spirit orb photos show energetic movement and sometimes contain faces or other shapes.

Levitation and Psychic Surgery

I was told years ago that I could levitate people, just like that without explanation. Within a few days, during a healing in a local park in Seattle, sure enough I was shown by Spirit exactly how to do it!

My client that day was a dear friend and a pranic healer. Right in the middle of the healing… up she went in her merkaba! I had no idea how this "levitation" would happen but when a client has a need for psychic surgery, the galactic and angelic teams will lift a person up either to my healing platform beyond the matrix or simply as high as they need to go for energetic purposes. It all depends on what needs to be accomplished for the client. The sitter goes up as far as they need to into the frequency needed for healing. The client may also hover over a body of water, a mountain or desert, depending on their need and ability to hold the frequency while getting adjusted. The levitation is felt in the mind as well as in the body. Clients have expressed they just do not want to come down! It's the ultimate in a peaceful experience to feel the Angels and galactic teams around you as the healing or surgery takes place.

Now What?

Nothing happened after a healing session. Or did it? What happens if you have finished working with a client and they report they felt nothing, zip, nada.

The first thing to remember is that every client experiences energy work in a different way. Some simply do not feel a thing until days later. These clients are integrating, and the energy can show up hours or days after healing. Some people need more time to not only physically integrate but emotionally and mentally integrate the work at a slower rate. Clients who are working on releasing overthinking, control or resistance may take more time to recognize something has happened during their healing. Some clients note that they were not used to "being in their bodies" and tend to take more time to feel a healing experience. It is important to remind clients to rest and hydrate after healing for several days. Remind them of what possible changes to look for such as relaxation, better mood, better sleep and reduction in pain or discomfort. Remember, a healer is just a cog in the machine, a beautiful part of the healing. The true healer is the client and if they are ready to heal and the timing is in place for it, the illness and condition will unlock.

CHAPTER 13:

5d and Beyond! Are We There Yet, Mom?

St Germain:
"You heard the call and woke up. Do not deny yourselves further. And if you are ready, as some will be, and more have already acknowledged the messages, you have begun the necessary changes and acknowledgment to self and others. I say, we are thankful for the partnering as we are unable to create the next steps without you."

Carl Jung:
"One who looks outside, dreams. One who looks inside, awakens. Let us expand on this today. Take no more time wondering if the connection between yourselves and those of us in the spirit realm is valid. Mediumship will always be valid. When mankind looks within it is a milestone, a time to celebrate."

Earth school is hard work, kids! Remember, you chose to come here and be a part of this Grand Awakening of the Human! You are tougher than you think.

When we arrived here on Earth on our birthday, we were square in the third dimension. As babies we didn't care about duality and materialism but since you are reading this book, I am sure you have noticed some of the games that are played here on Earth. Each dimension is a frequency.

Dimensions or planes within the spiritual realm

- 3D Earth separation, materialism, duality
- 4D astral, beginning awareness of universal law
- 5D no linear time, living from the heart, no judgment, unconditional love for our brothers and sisters
- 6D conscious of miracles, awareness of dimensional realms
- 7D Christ consciousness, galactic teaching and healing
- 8D full control of the "story" of life on Earth

- 9D full cosmic consciousness and stewardship of planet Earth
- 10D solar level
- 11D galactic golden ray, universal consciousness
- 12D unity consciousness

From the other side, my own mother reminded me that upon our awakening we now have a deeper sensitivity to see people within their pain rather than judging them. Humans judge everything! But once you awaken, the possibility of being aware of judgment, constantly coming up over and over will be the first step to becoming an observer.

Easy declarations to become the observer

- I declare that when I am judging something, I will begin to simply observe.
- I will follow my judgment back to its origin. Who first judged me? Why am I triggered now?
- I choose the observation stance.
- I prefer to observe rather than to judge.

This is a great start to begin to challenge your beliefs and habits.

When You are Awake, and Your Family is Not!

Newsflash! It's not your job to awaken people, not your friends and not your family. Pushing your point, even being extra excited about what's happening, may or may not send friends and family down the road to enlightenment.

No awakening soul is "higher up" or better in any way than an un-awakened person. We are simply waking at our own speed and timing. I liken it to a turkey with a timer that pops up when the turkey is done. Some turkeys have not popped their timers and worrying about them does not help and will just drive you crazy. A great conversation with no agenda may just open a closed mind. But certainly, a great conversation may just lead to new perspectives on both sides.

Humanity has been playing in a game of duality for thousands of years. The perception of who is in charge and making decisions has been a cover-up. The top few percent have kept the human race virtually stuck in the matrix. This becomes clear once awakening begins. We take responsibility for our own sovereignty. We will begin to learn our true creative power and know that working together; not separately, nor against others, who are our brothers and sisters, can create healing miracles and global change.

Believe in yourself first, then find others that believe in you.

Once I thought I had no one. I've always felt different, as if I didn't fit in. I was deep in meditation one day and I saw a great eagle flying towards me. She lifted me up. I was afraid! But soon she deposited me high up in the very top of a tree. There was fog all around me and I couldn't see anything. The eagle flew off and left me up there. Again, I was afraid until I heard the words "Reach out!"

When I lifted my hands, the fog cleared away and I saw many of my guide's faces all around me. They were very close, next to me all the time. This was a huge lesson. Of course, the eagle returned and gave me a soft and graceful landing.

The Schumann Resonance

Earth, herself, has a heartbeat or frequency called the Schumann Resonance. Sensitive people can feel the changes in Mother Earth's "heartbeat" and report being able to know when a storm is brewing or even earthquakes are about to happen.

As we awaken to our universal connections with all humans, our planet and our off-planet family, we may begin to feel more! We become even more attuned and willing to help Mother Earth, nature, animals and our brothers and sisters.

Assisting Planet Earth meditation

- Call in Creator God and your own Team of Light.
- Ground and re-calibrate.
- Focus on planet Earth and make the intention to send healing now.
- Imagine you are holding planet Earth just like a large globe on your lap while you sit in a beautiful, green field.
- Notice your breath and be sure your abdomen is rising on the "in" breath.
- Imagine that you are breathing emerald green healing light over the entire planet.
- After a few moments, change the color to gold and then to pink.
- Release Earth and notice how beautiful she looks!

Ascension Symptoms

During 2020, I heard over and over, "Why am I so tired? I feel like someone has unplugged my power cord." I heard about headaches like a little dragon sitting on one's head. Difficulty sleeping, nausea, pain and pressure everywhere and old issues coming back around again. Sometimes light coming into the physical vessel is a painful process. You, a big angel, are trying to fit in a human body!

All of these symptoms (assuming you have a ruled-out illness) can be credited to you becoming the new human or human 2.0. It's exciting! And if you can take the vantage point of these sensations are odd, but so exciting, you will do better and have an easier time getting through these human changes.

What the Heck are Those Numbers?

Every day I notice the time, morning and afternoon! 12:34! What the heck are these numbers? Easy, Spirit tells me, "one, two, three, four…GO!!!!" Do what you came to Earth this lifetime to do. Go for it! No time like the present. We are here now as an anchor for these divine incoming frequencies. For some angel numbers such as 1111 or 222 or 555 have long been noticed. Just what do they mean? These numbers hold angelic frequencies and carry certain meanings.

The number sequences can also be specific to a person. You might be drawn to license plates with numbers or even road signs. Really, anywhere at any time your light team can bring your awareness to single numbers and pairs of numbers or sequences. Dates are popular and show up often as messages from the deceased. Numbers carry vibrational frequencies especially on death days or birthdays. My own team shows me single numbers to quickly understand what is coming up for a client.

In my work, number one stands for new beginnings, two for healing, three for love and so on. There are universal meanings for certain numbers, but the message can go deeper. If you are constantly drawn to certain numbers or combinations, sit with your spirit team to find out what they would like to bring to your attention.

When it's time to awaken and connect with the universe, nothing can stop it! You are remembering who and what you are! Nothing around you looks the same. Synchronicities abound. Suddenly you've been noticing white feathers where none should be and know deep inside that this is a direct communication from your loved one on the other side.

I remember around the time of my father's passing, I found so many feathers it felt like he sent me a whole bird. I kept every one of them in my grandmother's old butter container. Synchronicities or "coincidences" can occur between people, or "déjà vu moments" may happen over and over during your awakening. Don't wait, ask for signs! Your team is waiting and so happy to show you these small tokens of love.

Hearing a song that has great meaning to you, that reminds you of a lost love and then immediately your old girlfriend calls you, is definitely a synchronicity. Or opening a special book to a random page and reading just the right passage that assists you with a problem that you couldn't figure out. It's a true sign that someone up there is looking out for you! You can believe it and take it to the bank.

We can all see with our own higher perception and we all have a small piece of the puzzle that is ascension. Just as stress and a busy brain can block healing, it can also block incoming messages and vision. Discernment is the key.

What is Universal Law

Many people have heard of the law of attraction. There is even an amazing movie about it called "The Secret." However, there are many universal laws. You may have even heard the phrase "as above, so below" or "as within, so without", this is also universal law!

In this book we show examples of three universal laws: the law of attraction, the law of resistance and the law of reflection. When we put the universal laws into place in our daily life, life just runs smoother. For example, the law of attraction proves that when our frequency aligns with the frequency of what we wish to bring or attract to ourselves, we get the job! Or the perfect partner or whatever we want.

You have probably heard the phrase "What one resists, persists." Control holds energy, whether it is a thought or words you say out loud over and over such as "I won't ever be free of this health problem." Our subconscious hears the words as resistance to health. Get in the habit of watching your words. This is the law of resistance.

Imagine judging your friend for his choice in a partner. The partner seems lazy to you. The law of reflection reminds us to focus on healing ourselves because what we notice in others is a reflection of us. Mirroring is easy to see one you begin to look for it.

Saint Francis of Assisi:
"There is the right side and another side. The law of the land and spiritual law. You are witnessing retooling and relabeling. This will not hold. There is only one law."

Quantum Entanglement

Science has proven that we are all connected. You may come to the understanding, as many people did in 2020, that pulling inside yourself and cocooning is needed. Very specific swaths of alone time are vital to bring yourself to the understanding of what is really important to you and what or who is ready to be released.
You may have found you needed fewer possessions and decided the clutter must go! Maybe you began to shop local, using up what you have, gifting, regifting, donating and recycling. Maybe you lost your taste for alcohol or certain foods. It goes along with awakening to your truest truth.

The Tired Fighter

Must we always react? No, but we are conditioned to fight. Put down your sword. Release that part of you that is the fighter. Why should we do this if it is also important to speak up? Because clear, direct communication heals us, but long held anger can cost you peace and your frequency.

Ascension will affect you whether or not you welcome it in ease or resist it. The light still comes in. When it comes in full force and then leaves, there can be debris left behind. Great troughs and great highs. This is something we all have to get used to.

Goddess Kali:
"One of the truths all must wake up to, is that yes, some people just do not like you! What an idea! Truly in our heart we know it's possible but when we realize that family, "friends" or workmates actually dislike us and wish us ill, it can be a shock. A shock as bright as illuminated truths can be.

Protect yourself, flow out your natural love, the ever-increasing energy on Earth will do the rest. Isn't that easy? Many make it so hard. Truths are simple by nature."

Chapter 14:

Contact, the Real Disclosure

Master Jesus tells us to welcome these glorious golden days of the awakening of our own higher self. Reason, wit, desire of knowledge and ultimate peace and enlightenment are ours for the taking. Morning has broken here on Earth. Live this time of awakening with full gusto, for time has changed and moved on. The fruit is service. Friendship and love is the bond.

> ***My mom, Vivian Skelly (from the other side):***
> *"Do not spend another moment wondering about planet Earth. It is the end of the game. See right behind that big dark cloud? That is the clear day. Of course one has to get through it. You can go two ways, become the bull or become the lamb, which will you be? A little of each, maybe. When you were a lamb, you got slaughtered until the moment of awakening. You were the receptacle of your family's anger and pain. Some are still sleeping but this is not your focus anymore. You are your own project. Rest and create."*

The real truth of disclosure comes down to average humans opening their hearts and meeting their star family halfway. We are also more than ready to understand our own true divinity and expanded abilities as we live from our hearts and not through our minds.

Meeting Your Own Star Family

I met my first galactic guide, a Sirian named Entirah-meh, during an activation with another healer. The Sirian stood in a circle with me along with the rest of my guidance team. The galactic energy was cool in temperature and high and light, like being in the presence of angels. The information he has given to me over the years has been nothing but the truth.

Discerning Truth

Feel into your channeling or message. Does it make you feel positive and ring true? We as humans are receivers and transmitters. Though we have a short attention span radio, we have the ability to tune in! From the star beings' vantage point, they wish to assist us as they have heard our suffering.

Ships Incoming!

Even today, as news of spacecraft and photos come in from all over the world, Ufologists are still trotting out old photos and information from Roswell, New Mexico from back in the day. There is no place in the new reality for ego, fear, competition and being stuck in an old narrative regarding our galactic brothers and sisters. It's time to know they've always been right here with us. They are actually us.

Anyone can meet their galactic friends and family if you connect with them by holding love in your heart and keeping your mind open. Make a statement through your higher self that you are ready to meet them. I met the second galactic being at a conference. I was taken to a ship and met the Galactic Federation of Light. I have been in conscious contact with them regularly since that meeting.

The Celestial Blue Beings

"As the blue light flows over Earth, peace is felt. The light will progress over time. Continue to hold the blue light over your planet. Call us in and make us a part of your life. There are many souls on Earth that we work with already, who know us as their divine counterparts. As the days go forward, signs of strength, creation and service will evolve past anything seen on Earth before. We are ready."

If you wish to know more about the Celestial Blue Beings, please visit Nancy Rebecca's Facebook page, "Blue Light Movement." Nancy teaches us to ground into the blue crystal core of the Earth.

The ECETI Ranch, Enlightened Contact with Extraterrestrial Intelligence

I count myself fortunate to live just 3 1/2 hours away from Trout Lake, Washington, the home of the ECETI Ranch. Contact happens every day in this beautiful place near Mount Adams. I've been there twice to take part in a group adventure with like-minded friends. We were overwhelmed at the number of ships in the skies at night above the ranch and over Mount Adams. Once you visit the ranch, you'll never stop looking up! I've seen several UFOs in my life: one near Seattle and a few in my hometown of Tacoma, Washington. Now they are so easy to spot.

> *Sirian Council:*
>
> *"Listen, for we speak to you in so many ways. Obviously, we can adjust your frequency and heal if you ask us to but look up! We are speaking to you all day in the skies for those who can hear and see. Ask us to be present for healing. Ask us for words and we shall speak. All shall know our pure intention as healers and the ones who will help to bring together peace on New Earth. This world is grand and becoming lighter. Dive into this light, beloved brothers and sisters. Treat yourself to the light in the early morning.*

Can you see how close we are to you in just an instant. This is our connection with you. When we say family ship, we mean it. We are your family, we are you. Tell all about your experience. Many are hearing the call. The light expansion is upon you!"

Commander Ashtar:
"I am with you tonight for a reason. This place is a place of love for you. Feel it well. When you're not in a place of love, you will compare and release the other places and people. We wish to show you the ships."

Grandmother Spider

At the ECETI Ranch, I took part in a past life regression, led by hypnotist and past life regressionist Lori Aletha. Our group focused on viewing several past lifetimes where we had all been together in Atlantis. Lori told us that sometimes we feel unreasonable fear. We must go back to the original time when the trauma occurred so that we can reach our full potential in this lifetime. Many of us received messages during the regression at ECETI. In my vision, I was able to see all of us as a group weaving a tri-level web over Earth, on and inside Earth itself. This vision showed the true meaning of the universal law "as above, so below." Many of us in the group are soul family. We are back together again this lifetime to bring in the light through our grid point.

Pleiadian Guide Blue:
"Each shall perceive and experience Ascension in their own way. Do not wonder or worry."

The Angelic Realm

Who are the Holy Ones? Spirit, ascended masters and beings from the light. You are a holy, divine being, equal to those held in esteem for millennia. It is now time to know this truth. We cannot and they cannot get as much done without one another. When we are ready to work through our higher selves and recognize our I AM Presence, we are ready to release all of the old beliefs and big structures that have held it in place for eons. This matrix includes religion, birth family, institutions, news and more! This is no time for a guru! All that you need is within YOU! Love answers every question, now what do you need to know?

Over the years I have spoken to so many ascended masters and hierarchy, various deceased musicians, deceased presidents, holy ones from every realm. Why are they here now and in such numbers? Because we are ready. They have heard our pleas and are ready, we just have to ask for help.

Do you remember when you first realized you had a guardian angel? Or the day you were touched by the Holy Spirit or in the presence of your guide? I remember the evening I saw a gigantic angel in my mom's and dad's house. I didn't know Archangel Gabriel at the time. I asked my mom if she could see it. She said "No, but I can see that you can." At that moment, I just needed someone to believe me. It helped me to give over to complete belief and assurance in the Holy Ones. Sometimes I felt they were the only ones that loved me in my darkest days.

Your Guardian Angel

Holy Mother Mary:
"Do you know the answer inside your heart of hearts where we reside together and dance with the stars? It is where it all began, after all. We are all dust from a beautiful source. Take me with you forever, I'm never apart from you. I go where you go. You are not alone and never have been. Angels surround you. Do not fear, as I have told you. Make your moves through your heart and you will not go wrong."

We all have a guardian angel that stays with us throughout our life. Angels protect, serve and get things done. The best way to describe this realm is that you'll know it by its love frequency.

Albert Einstein:
"Creator God loved us so much, the angels were created to prove this!"

Guardian angels choose who they look after over a lifetime or many lifetimes. Children often know them as their very first playmate. Angels also can be thought of as a bridge between humans and Creator. As the frequency on Earth rises, and our frequency rises too, we are meant to work directly with those celestial beings.

Guardian angels can intercede if it looks like we are just about to make a huge misstep or get into trouble. If we are not meant to have a catastrophe per our blueprint, sometimes an accident is just an accident. There are many photos and stories proving the intercession of celestial beings at just the right moment. People report seeing energetic halos of light around those who just *happen* to show up and then poof! They easily disappear.

Many sensitive people can hear the sound of wings or sense the frequency of angels. There are people alive on Earth today who are Earth Angels and have come from their angelic families to be here, now; for lessons and the great healing of humanity and planet Earth.

Some of us on Earth are in a familial line of Seraphim described as direct caretakers of the throne of God. We can be from the realm of angels of justice, archangels (or God's messengers) and so on. We are here on planet Earth to anchor those divine energies just by being who we are. We can think of the angels and ascended masters as the hierarchy or "upper management," but they wish to be known as our ascension partners.

Angels are celestial beings who intercede between God and humans. Light is their hallmark as well as the sense of wings and halos of light. The angels hold different jobs or levels.

- Seraphim are direct caretakers of the throne of God.

- Cherubim are the guardians.

- Thrones are justices.

- Dominions assist authority in government.

- Virtues foretell future or miracles and assist in healing.

- Powers are the defending angels and have control over seasons.
- Principalities command lower angels and raise us humans up.
- Archangels are God's messengers.

Who are the Archangels?

Most people know at least a few of the archangels as they appear in the writings of several religions. Here are a few that I work with every day:

- Archangel Michael is a warrior protector of righteousness and mercy. With his sword of light, he clears fear and releases us from bonds.
- Archangel Raphael, with his emerald ray, heals us physically and emotionally. He brings in harmony and peace.
- Archangel Gabriel of the diamond ray is a messenger of God. This Archangel assists writers and teachers.
- Archangel Metatron's golden ray guides humanity. This archangel is involved in forming sacred geometry and is aligned with the great awakening of Earth.

Archangel Michael:
"I am Michael, always with you. Please to instruct all to reach out to me. I will come when my name is invoked in peace, fear, love, reverence or most importantly, right now at this time on Earth, friendship. It is a time past duality as we are truly one on planet Earth. You will see the return of the masters, angels and star beings, gods and goddesses of all realms to work together for growth of the human race. All together as one. Not until this moment could it happen. Humanity has reached the tipping point for this to occur. Fear and peace, anger and love, want and need, and wealth beyond need, co exists at this moment.

There will be a time of separation of worlds of frequency. It has begun to happen and continues, but my point is, your heart is the vehicle to determine which world you will reside in. We shall assist in great heart openings worldwide, all of us shall be pointed towards that end. Grace for all, always. Would it make sense for abandonment, even at the last breath? No, at the last breath, a human can discover the truth of who they truly are, a divine being of light unto oneself. It is so hard for some to wrap their minds around it. Many live in fear and feel unworthy of the love of God. To find it in one's own heart is the way.

You have a responsibility to speak out when you see or hear injustices. You know in your heart of hearts it must be done. Say the word and we shall assist. It is not for you to worry or wonder, simply you are one bead on the chain. Create a board of names and hold them in the energy each day. Do this and change will occur."

Universal Angel Holy Mother Mary:
"You are held in my love every moment of your life. I am the link between God and child. I'm a balm for your heart."

I saw Holy Mother Mary one afternoon in Seattle while meditating. I used to sit by a bedroom window in my old house and I happened to look outside when I came back into my body after meditation. I saw her outside of the second-floor window of my home. I didn't know until 25 years later that she is my guardian angel. Holy Mother Mary was my very first teacher along with Clara Barton of the Red Cross.

Dark Night of the Soul

During Lionsgate, in August 2019 and 2020, I had a transformational death or Phoenix death. I was exhausted and ill. I had to make a decision to stay in this avatar body here on Earth. I was contacted twice in visions by Holy Mother Mary. She appeared in one vision where I saw all of my guides that are very close to me inside a house. I was sitting on the front porch. It was so peaceful! Seventh Heaven.

I needed guidance to understand this vision and later with help, I understood that my guides were checking on me. Every once in a while, coming out on the porch, in effect to say "Are you okay out there? Would you like to come back in?"

I learned that I had not released grief around the loss of my mother and father. It was explained to me that my body was crying. These emotions needed to come out, we need not wait until the end of our lives to look back on what has been painful.

Jesus Christ:
"You are now on a road by yourself. Take your days in the desert now. Sit within the fire and be free. Learn these lessons as all hearts are not of love."

Robert Frost:
"You have been listening to silence for a reason. We want you to be completely ready to sit with us without distraction. If you are ready now, let's begin."

The Elemental Realm

The Elemental Realm, or spirits of Earth, includes fairies, trolls, gnomes, dragons and mermaids. These beings guard sacred sites and are great healers. In fact, think of how great you feel after a day in the forest. The elemental realm is responsible for that frequency you are feeling.

Dragons and unicorns are our energetic allies. Dragons assist us in fetching information and can help us to raise our vibration and protect us. They are from the fourth dimension. Unicorns carry the highest rainbow angelic light. I regularly work with two.

I took a trip to Mount Shasta in the fall of 2019. I had in mind to find a portal that everyone talks about as the door into inner Earth or Telos. My guide is St. Germain, and he is associated with Mount Shasta where there have been many sightings of the violet flame. Adama of Telos is the high priest of the mountain. I was hoping I would feel something special on the mountain and I did! I could feel the vibration of both of these beautiful guides. The energy of the mountain is tremendous. Power and peace.

I had a vision of animals singing across the river during a morning meditation. I could see rainbow ships coming in. As we walked up the trail into the field, I searched for the doorway. Once I relaxed, I understood a doorway was before me in a tree. I entered in and met the Inner Earth guides.

Ra and Seventh Heaven

My guide, Ra, showed me a vision of the intersection of two walls. He told me to walk through the corner where the two walls came together. I entered what I knew to be Seventh Heaven or Seventh Dimension. Many elementals and animals greeted me. I sat under a beautiful tree and looked down at my body. My skin was blue.

Gods and Goddesses

Gods and Goddesses were some of the first creators of civilizations across Earth. Early humans called upon their pantheon in times of struggle and celebration. Gods and Goddesses from the Greek, Egyptian, Babylonian, Mayan, Norse, as well as others, show up when I work with people whose soul's origin can be found in these realms. I have had the pleasure to work with Quan Yin, Athena, Osiris, Ra, Thoth, The Morrigan, Hecate and many more. The sheer energy when working with this realm is extraordinary. The sons and daughters of this realm on Earth today are forces to be reckoned with, true creator beings.

Goddess Athena

"Call us in. Make us a part of your life. We have so many souls on Earth at work with us already who know us as their divine counterparts. As days go forward, signs of strength, creation and service will evolve past anything seen on Earth. As for us, we are ready to work with you to build and heal."

Chapter 15:

Using The Codes

Jesus Christ:
"When you support what can be done and what is possible, you draw in those who are willing. When one holds fear, one draws in the struggle and the struggling."

As healers, we lovingly assist those who seek us out for healing. There must be willingness to change when the client steps forward.

Boosting the Codes

Congratulations! You have made the decision to learn how to work with the Angelic Healing and Regenerative Codes!

These light codes were implanted in my DNA during the time of Lemuria, which existed before and during the time of Atlantis. The transfer from teacher to student or client is held by Archangel Metatron, the Seraphim, the Arcturians and Ascended Master Kuthumi.

In this chapter, we introduce the codes and describe how they work when they are entered into the body of a human or animal.

In class, in person or online, I describe how to release the codes from the body of the instructor into the student. It is a process that must be worked with over a two-day period. This process is called "the boost." A group of codes entering the body is called a "stream."

In order to work with the light codes, one must take the class, learn to use the codes, receive the transfer or boost and develop the frequency that is needed to use them over a two-day period. The transfer of the stream of codes is sacred and must be completed in class.

Healing in person or over distance or passing the codes to a student:

- Hold the frequency of love.

- Call in Creator and your Team of Light.

- Ground and clear yourself as well as the space you are working in.

- Call in the client or student and call in their Team of Light or have the student set their own intention.

- Intend to receive the visualization of the path and template.

- Walk on the path towards the template.

- Call in the Seven Galactic Suns, see the golden light shine down through our portal Sun, visualize the light pulsing down through you as the teacher and through the student or client, and down into the Earth where it continues until it aligns with the Inner Earth Sun at the core of the Earth.

- Return your consciousness to the template. See or imagine your bare feet on the color of the path that has come to you when you ask for the path and template.

- If you are using the codes to heal yourself or sending the codes by distance healing to a client, or boosting the codes into a student, view each code one by one and hold the image in your mind.

- Say the code's name out loud.

- Use the pendulum to ask if the code has transferred and if you need to, tap the code in more than once.

- If the code has transferred, go onto the next code.

- If you are passing the entire code stream to a student, view the codes one by one and hold each in your mind and say its name.

What to watch for during a healing:

- Changes in breathing
- Shifting the body
- Emotions
- Responses to questions
- The code may need to be "tapped in" several times, if the client is having resistance.

Some clients and students may feel nothing, they may notice changes later or feel emotional and physical changes right away. Everyone is different.

What to watch for when passing the Codes to a student:

- Changes in breathing
- Shifting the body

- Emotions
- Responses to questions
- How your body is feeling as the codes are being sent from you into the student.
- The animation of the codes.

Each code has a specific job. There are eight specific titles to a group of three, four or five, depending on the codes.

The Codes Work in the Following Way:

Prepare
1. Power Up! (Let's Do This!)
2. Begin
3. Prepare
4. Open (Time, Space, Matter)

Clear Energetic Field
5. Zero Point (Create)
6. Start (Go)
7. Clear (Energetic Field)
8. Stabilize (Grounding)
9. Return (Sovereignty)

The Heart Opens
10. Expand (Heart Field)
11. Open (Love Others)
12. Release (Grief)
13. Release (Depression)

Release
14. Release (Pain Body)
15. Release (Anxiety)
16. Open (Self Love)
17. Begin (Flow)
18. Release (Control, Fight or Flight)

Release
19. Release (Roadblocks)
20. Release (Thought Forms)
21. Release (Collective Emotions)
22. Release (Struggle With Others)

Build Up
23. Move On (Get Up)
24. Claim (Stand Your Ground)
25. Receive (Self Worth)
26. Rise (Take Your Place)

Moving On
27. Move (Progress)
28. Breakthrough (Perfectionism)
29. Accelerate (New Path)
30. Release (Mirroring)

Final Adjustment
31. Release (Bullying)
32. Boost (Ease, Not Debt)
33. Equal (Looping)

The healing and regenerative codes can be combined with any other type of alternative or metaphysical modality. I use the codes every day on myself and send them out to clients in each reading and healing that I do.

The codes may be experienced as relaxing and even "nap producing". Remind your client or students to listen to their body and rest as their energy field adjusts to this healing. After several times of receiving the codes, the body adjusts past the need to nap, retains the relaxed feeling, and will notice all of the rest of the positive results over time.

Congratulations! Thank you for going on this journey through a brand-new modality with me! This first book is a step into the future of healing and will in time evolve as new codes show themselves.

THE *art* OF YOUR ENERGY

Prepare

1. Power Up!

2. Begin

3. Prepare

4. Open

THE *art* OF YOUR ENERGY

Clear The Energetic Field

5. Zero Point
Create (Time, Space, Matter)

6. Start
Go!

7. Clear
Energetic Field

8. Stabilize
Ground

9. Return
Sovereignty

THE *art* OF YOUR ENERGY

The Heart Opens

10. Expand
Heart Field

11. Open
To Love Others

12. Release
Grief

13. Release
Depression

Release

14. Release
Pain Body

15. Release
Anxiety

16. Open
Self Love

17. Begin
Flow

18. Release
Control (Fight/Flight), Cording

Release

19. Release
Road Block

20. Release
Thought Forms

21. Release
Collective Emotions

22. Release
Struggle With Others, Ancestral

THE *art* OF YOUR ENERGY

Build Up

23. Move On
Get Up

24. Claim
Stand Your Ground

25. Receive
Self Worth

26. Rise
Take Your Place

Moving On

27. Move
Progress - Release Shackles

28. Breakthrough
Release Perfectionism

29. Accelerate
New Path

30. Release
Mirroring

THE *art* OF YOUR ENERGY

Final Adjustment

31. Release
Bullying

32. Boost
Ease Not Debt

33. Equal
Looping

THE *art* OF YOUR ENERGY

Prepare

1. Power Up!

2. Begin

3. Prepare

4. Open

Clear The Energetic Field

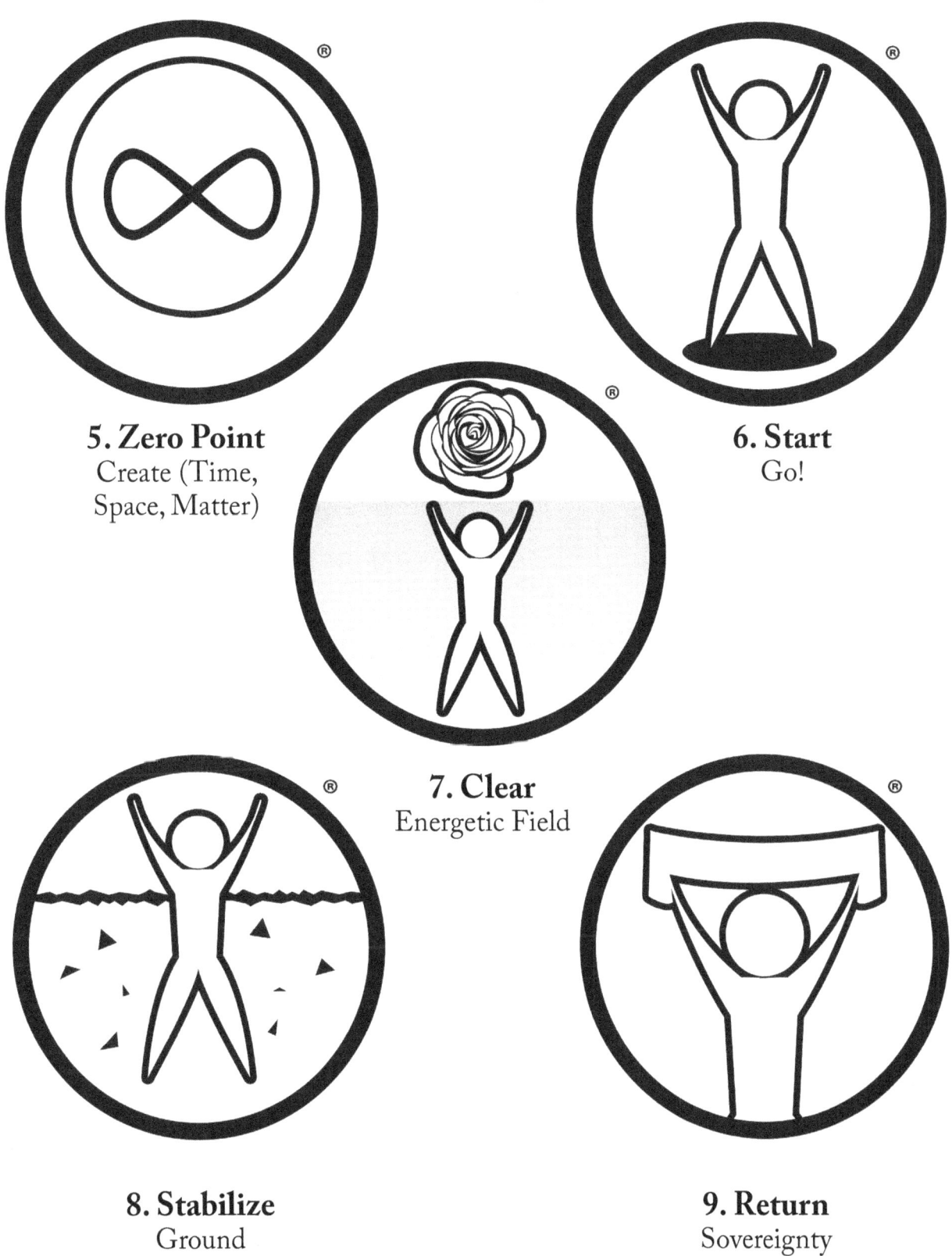

5. Zero Point
Create (Time, Space, Matter)

6. Start
Go!

7. Clear
Energetic Field

8. Stabilize
Ground

9. Return
Sovereignty

The Heart Opens

10. Expand
Heart Field

11. Open
To Love Others

12. Release
Grief

13. Release
Depression

Release

14. Release
Pain Body

15. Release
Anxiety

16. Open
Self Love

17. Begin
Flow

18. Release
Control (Fight/Flight), Cording

Release

19. Release
Road Block

20. Release
Thought Forms

21. Release
Collective Emotions

22. Release
Struggle With Others, Ancestral

THE *art* OF YOUR ENERGY

Build Up

23. Move On
Get Up

24. Claim
Stand Your Ground

25. Receive
Self Worth

26. Rise
Take Your Place

Moving On

27. Move
Progress - Release Shackles

28. Breakthrough
Release Perfectionism

29. Accelerate
New Path

30. Release
Mirroring

Final Adjustment

31. Release
Bullying

32. Boost
Ease Not Debt

33. Equal
Looping

Thank you

Every writer has help when a book is written and this one took a village, celestial and terrestrial.

First off, I'd like to thank my Team of Light, my Companion Guide and Robert the Writer (in Spirit).

Thank you to my publisher, Doce Blant Publishing and editor Patricia Brack.

Thank you to my husband, Thomas Beckman, for believing in this project and for the artful creation of the Light Codes. The Codes were channeled from Spirit and Thom brought them to life.

This book was an exercise in trust, belief in myself and the power of the human energetic field. I learned to absolutely trust that the moment when I needed to know something, the Holy Ones would step in. They never let me down.

Thank you to the metaphysicians who inspired the words in several releasing and armoring affirmations. Thank you to the healers who allowed me to quote them: Derek Condit, Tracy Kelly Williams, Lola Singer, Michiko Hayashi for Dr. Masaru Emoto, and Jenny Grace.

Thank you to my clients and friends who made up the original test lists and List of Love 100.

You helped me to understand how powerful and life changing these Light Codes truly are. May God bless you all.

And lastly, my thanks goes out to medium and author Lou J. Free, who taught so many of us to watch out for signs. Lori Aletha, for inspiration, Ann Muckerjie from our Facebook page Hands of Light and over 1000 healers and pray-ers that assist our community on Hands of Light everyday (join us!), my Shasta Sisters, Melanie Long from Inter Dimension (for the bigger picture); Cori Bodily, MS, DC, CN; and Kirsty Docken, EAMP, LAc, MSOM, MASLP for loving care of this avatar body. My heartfelt thank-you goes to my soul family. Thank you for loving me.

Metaphysicians

**Tracy Kelly Williams, Medium and Dream Teacher,
Soul Mentorship and Energetic Practitioner**
Dream Yourself Awake on Facebook
www.onewithallbeings.net

Derek Condit, Intuitive/Clairvoyant, Energy Healer
Shungite Retailer
Mystical Wares
17869-WA 536
Mount Vernon, Wa. 98273
www.mysticalwares.net

Rev. Lola Singer, Light Language Artist and Singer
Usui Reiki Master, CHIOS Energy Master/Teacher
www.lightlanguagearts.com

Michiko Hayashi, Emoto Peace Project
Messages From Water
www.emotopeaceproject.net
epp@EmotoPeaceProject.net

Jenny Grace, Clairvoyant Healer
www.intuitivevillage.com
www.facebook.com/IntuitiveVillage

Lori Aletha, Cht
Past Life Regressionist and Certified Hypnotherapist, Producer of Northwest Psychic Fairs
lori@liveloveshare@gmail.com

Nancy Rebecca, RN, Clairvoyant Healer
Intuitive Mind Center
www.intuitivemind.org
Facebook: Blue Light Movement
www.facebook.com/groups/727301044289645

www.ingramcontent.com/pod-product-compliance
Lightning Source LLC
Chambersburg PA
CBHW082039080526
44578CB00009B/749